BERNARD PORTER is Emeritus Professor of History at the University of Newcastle. He has also taught at the universities of Cambridge, Hull, Yale, Sydney, Stockholm and Copenhagen. He has published ten books before this one, many of them on imperial themes, including *Critics of Empire*, *The Lion's Share* and *The Absent-Minded Imperialists*. He also contributes regularly to the *London Review of Books*, the *Guardian* and other journals.

'Bernard Porter writes in a clear and engaging manner and does not hesitate to take on some of the most difficult and controversial issues'

Wm. Roger Louis, Kerr Professor of English History and Culture, The University of Texas at Austin

'Bernard Porter writes with the authority and verve one has come to expect from an author of a number of books on the history of the British Empire. This one is short, pointed, iconoclastic and highly readable. He makes the point that the "the British Empire is misunderstood in popular mythology", and in clarifying why this is so, he succeeds wonderfully well. Porter's *British Imperial* is sure-handed and confident and his publication is to be welcomed and celebrated.'

C. Brad Faught, Professor of History, Tyndale University College

BRITISH IMPERIAL

WHAT THE EMPIRE WASN'T

BERNARD PORTER

I.B. TAURIS
LONDON · NEW YORK

Published in 2016 by
I.B. Tauris & Co. Ltd
London • New York
www.ibtauris.com

ISBN: 978 1 78453 445 5
eISBN: 978 0 85773 957 5

A full CIP record for this book is available from the British Library
A full CIP record is available from the Library of Congress

Library of Congress Catalog Card Number: available

Text designed and typeset by Tetragon, London
Printed and bound in Sweden by Scandbook

MIX
Papper från
ansvarsfulla källor
FSC
www.fsc.org
FSC® C007584

Contents

For Jasmine, Sid, Allie,
Tegan, Edie, Mary and Sonja:
when they're old enough to read it.

Introduction

THE BRITISH EMPIRE is so misunderstood. Not by serious students of it, necessarily, but in popular mythology. The idea for this book first came to me when I was once asked by a fellow guest at a party in Sweden, who had learned what I work on – I usually try to keep it quiet, but she was insistent: 'Why on earth did you' – she meant Britain, not me personally, I think – '*want* an empire?' For a good Social Democrat that seemed difficult to understand. Of course it is, put in that way. I can't remember exactly how I replied to her, except to regurgitate some of the research I had been writing up recently that seemed to show that people generally in Britain *didn't* want one, particularly. That, however, didn't answer the underlying question, which now became: if most of you were indifferent about your empire, why did it come about nonetheless? That deserved a fuller explanation than I was able to offer over *sill* and *aquavit* at a generally light-hearted occasion in a suburb of Stockholm. Hence this short book. The idea of it is to pre-empt future questions like my fellow guest's, which arise from a series of basic misconceptions of the subject. Of course Britain didn't acquire her empire because she 'wanted' one. It was more complicated than that.

That may be uncharacteristic of empires generally. This might be one of our problems: that the word 'empire' immediately suggests comparisons with other historical empires, which tend to stick. The main ones in Britain's historical memory are the Roman, which she was part of, and the Napoleonic, which she successfully resisted. Both of those were the results of conquest by men – 'emperors' – who set out to conquer, deliberately. The word itself also has a strong and positive resonance, deriving as it does from the Latin *imperium*, which meant power or authority. Together, and encouraged by late-nineteenth-century imperialists who rather liked these analogies (the first one, at any rate; the second was too close for comfort), this puffed up the image of the British Empire into something quite different from the reality. Later the fault was compounded by left- and right-wing analyses of British imperialism which painted it, on the one hand, as an unconscionable evil – capitalist, racist, even genocidal – and on the other as the means by which Britain helped 'civilise', or 'modernise', the world. That is generally what the popular British debate about imperialism focuses on today. My take on it is that both sides are mistaken, because they get the whole nature of the phenomenon wrong.

Here is my understanding of most *other* people's understanding of the old British Empire today. (I may be wrong; I've not talked to everyone.) It was big – a quarter of the earth's land surface and a fifth of its population: or was it the other way around? – and powerful. It was what made Britain a 'Great Power'. It went back in time to the Elizabethans – so it was pretty durable. It was accumulated by 'imperialists', as a matter of policy. It was cheered on by the people. It either reflected, or else permeated, British culture and society. It sought to impose British ways on everyone it ruled; all who could benefit from them, that is, because it also tended to be racist, and so to exclude 'inferior races', who were to be eradicated, or enslaved, or – the best hope for them – looked after for aeons like children. It was exploitative, often brutally so. In the end, however, it was dissolved voluntarily, calmly and mainly peacefully. Finally, it had a great and lasting impact on the world, either for good or for ill. As a consequence it should be a matter either of pride for us Britons today, or of shame. Is that fair? If not I may be setting up straw dolls. But it still may be worth examining the reality of British imperialism against them, using them as benchmarks or touchstones, for emphasis and clarity. They are not all entirely wrong, incidentally. That is not usually the way with historical analyses. It is why historians are so often and so infuriatingly equivocal when they are asked to adjudicate on areas of their expertise: 'Well, yes, in a way, *but*…' A number of my ideas will be along those lines; the point being, of course, that the 'but' is crucially important. And then, of course, there is the possibility that I might be wrong. (A number of scholars think I am on the subject of 'popular imperialism'.) That must always be borne in mind.

What I aim to do in this book is to examine the phenomenon of British imperialism critically, by, firstly, contextualising it, against the background of contemporary British society, the situation of the world, and rival or complementary historical forces; and secondly, deconstructing it, in the sense of breaking it down into its constituent components. All this needs to be done in order to counter the common trend today to lump so many disparate things together under the name of imperialism, and then to account for them simply in terms of that word, as though the notion of 'imperialism' contained a sufficient explanation on its own without any further examination being necessary. ('Oh, that's American imperialism.' Full stop.) Some years ago I suggested at a conference that we imperial historians agree to a moratorium on the 'e', 'i' and 'c' words – 'empire', 'imperial', 'colonial', and so on – for, say five years, forcing us to see if we couldn't understand our subject more, or at least differently, without them. No one, so far as I can tell, took any notice of this, and in any case the five years is now up, so I won't be following my own advice in this book; but I shall endeavour to delve behind the 'e', 'i' and 'c' words whenever I can. A disadvantage of this approach may be that it complicates things – it's much easier if we put them all in one 'imperial' basket – but isn't that, after all, one of the purposes of serious history? And complex doesn't necessarily mean difficult. I've aimed for a clear exposition and approachable style in what follows – it wasn't difficult; it's how I usually write before po-faced editors come in to 'correct' me – with even a few jokes. I'm sure I'll get some stick for the latter. One of my previous books was once banned by a southern American state school board for one; it made light fun of Christianity. But I'm too old and unambitious now to care.

Because it's mainly an 'ideas' book, and pretty short, there won't be much narrative in it – just a bit, to give the bare outlines of the story, and for flavour. This is partly to make the ideas stand out more clearly; and partly because I have already written my narrative account, in *The Lion's Share*, now in its fifth edition, to which readers are of course directed if that's what they want. They might also take a look at my *Empire Ways*, a collection of essays to be published at roughly the same time as this, which is even more flavoursome. Or, if they prefer something more up-to-date and (I think) better, to a couple of quite recent books by others, which are the first to be cited in the Bibliography.

The other caveat, or warning, I should issue at the start – a more important one – is that this is a very one-sided view of British imperialism. By that I don't mean that it is judgementally biased – I think that readers will find it is far from that – but that it deals with the subject from a metropolitan British point of view, rather than that of Britain's colonial subjects. It is, in other words, an account of British imperial*ism* – its sources, motives, methods, and so on – rather than of the British *Empire* as such. The latter would have required far more detail and analysis of how colonial peoples were *affected* by imperialism, how they lived under the British flag in the Gold Coast or Bengal or New Zealand, for example, or without the British flag in places that were merely informally dominated by Britain, which – although I have read plenty of the secondary literature about this, and have kept that in mind in what follows – I have never *researched* to the extent that would make me feel confident about generalising in this area. A colonial view of the Empire at any time was bound to diverge from a metropolitan one, while being, of course, just as valid. The same is true of its history. But these are complementary perspectives, not alternatives. They can inform each other. If you are at the barrel end of a gun, it is useful to know what is happening at the butt.

Lastly, readers may be puzzled by the references to Sweden here. Sweden was not one of the leading European imperial powers in the period covered by this book, which may make this seem anomalous. My excuses are that I live there much of the time, and was started off on this enterprise there, as I explained at the beginning of this Introduction; but also that it never does any harm to look at even narrow national histories from a wider perspective. 'What should they know of England who only England know?' asked Kipling once. He meant something entirely different – he was complaining about his compatriots' ignorance of their empire – but it could be taken as a general rule for historians. (It's why British school history syllabuses should never focus on Britain, *or* the Empire, alone.) You can only understand one set of historical experiences by looking at it from the vantage point of another. Both I and my Swedish partner ('*sambo*': a startling term to a British imperial historian) have modified our views of our own countries' histories by looking at them from the other's perspective. As a result, she no longer believes that social democracy is the 'normal' state of humankind. That means it has to be *explained* in Sweden. I can say the same about imperialism. It was my fleeting Swedish acquaintance at Gösta and Lena's party who brought that home to me. Hence this book.

Readers will find it very lightly referenced. This is because to back up many of the statements made here would involve an enormous *apparatus criticus*, which I feel would make the book unwieldy. I am, however, very conscious of the duty required of writers, and especially academic writers, to provide evidence for all their historical claims, and to indicate to readers where this can be found, so that they can check. Here I have restricted my specific endnotes to facts and quotations that cannot be easily verified. In addition to this, I have appended to each chapter a bibliography of some of the works that will provide general sources that should be helpful. A few feature my own earlier works. (It seemed to me that simply citing *The Absent-Minded Imperialists* was preferable to reproducing again all the many sources on which chapter 6 is based.) Better-known facts can easily be checked, these days, via Google and Wikipedia (though I'm too old and traditional myself to rely on the latter absolutely). I recommend readers to do so if they're not sure. Again, I'm bound to be wrong on many – hopefully minor – things.

My publishers, I.B. Tauris, and especially Lester Crook, should head my brief list of acknowledgements; brief because to catalogue the names of every person and every institution that has contributed to the nearly fifty years of research, reading and writing that this book is based on would be impossible. If I did, the list would begin with some of my early teachers and tutors (Alan Mould, Peter Watkins, Patrick Bury, John Roach, Ronald Robinson); some wonderful students at Cambridge, Hull, Newcastle, Yale and Sydney universities; and my successive families – my former wife Deirdre and our children, and my beloved *sambo* Kajsa and her children ('*bonusbarn*'). But it was Lester who inspired, commissioned and fought for this book. I hope it isn't felt to let him and I.B.Tauris down. Lastly, after searching for three years for the unnamed person who asked me that question at Gösta and Lena's party, I finally found her again. It happened when the book was at the copy-editing stage, and quite fortuitously. She gave us a lift back from another of Gösta and Lena's parties. Thank you so much, Anna Sundberg, for starting this whole thing off.

ONE

Hybridity

BRITISH IMPERIALISM was a two-headed monster. Often the two heads pulled in different ways. It also had a torso, which was by and large indifferent to what either of the heads was doing, and a tail that occasionally wagged in protest against both of them. That may be stretching this particular metaphor somewhat. Tails don't usually wag in protest. As well as this, British imperialism had many other aspects which can't be easily identified with or included in any of these parts: left head, right head, body, tail. It was a complex phenomenon, which has too often been oversimplified for propaganda reasons, or, more innocently, in order to render it easier to understand. My 'monster' analogy is, I admit, intended to do the latter, but should be taken with the proviso that it is only one way of looking at British imperialism; which I think should be revealing, but will still leave many things unexplained.

The reason why British imperialism was two-headed (at least) is that the society it sprang from was a hybrid one. The form of the hybridity has been known to historians for years. Contemporaries were aware of it too. Britain started as a feudal, aristocracy-dominated couple of nations, but then was transformed into a single capitalist, middle-class-dominated one. The stages by which this happened need not detain us here; except to say that it was not a consistent process, and it was never quite completed until – arguably – our own time. This is what accounted for Britain's 'hybridity' in the eighteenth, nineteenth and much of the twentieth centuries, with capitalism always evolving and advancing – no one today, surely, can doubt that it has been the major and most powerful progressive force in modern world history – but in fits and starts, and with the old ways and the social classes associated with them often resisting and fighting back. In the nineteenth century, in particular, which is the period most associated with the British Empire, neither was completely dominant. Reforms of the parliamentary franchise were giving more and more power to the middle classes. But, in terms of personnel and institutions, the upper classes still ruled. This dichotomy is central to an understanding of the imperialism of that time: the nineteenth century, and around fifty years on either side of it. Capitalism and feudalism were the two heads of the monster. But they didn't always agree. Sometimes they snapped at each other. Which helps explain the inconsistencies and contradictions of British imperial policy and practice throughout this period; and also, incidentally, why the anti-imperialist tail didn't wag more than it did.

Almost every nation has been 'imperialistic' at one time or another. I sometimes chaff my supposedly innocent Swedish friends with this: the Vikings; Swedish expansion in the Baltic during the *Stormaktstiden* (roughly the second half of the seventeenth century); the colonisation of Norrland, western Finland and Minnesota; an East India Company like Britain's; quite a few overseas colonies, including a Caribbean one that was still practising slavery twenty years after it was abolished in the British Empire; the union with Norway; individual Swedes employed by colonial regimes all over Africa; and (using the word rather more loosely) the global spread of IKEA. That's my response when the Swedes start taunting me with being an 'imperialist', because I'm British. It is not a purely national characteristic. It goes back to prehistoric times, obviously, otherwise we would still all be crowded together in the Rift Valley of Kenya, and there would be more Neanderthals about. From then until the beginning of modern times peoples have always expanded, usually at the expense of other peoples, following a number of different imperatives: land-hunger, labour-hunger (slavery), fleeing from natural catastrophes, avarice, the sex drive, adventure, the aggressive gene that may be in all of us (all men, at any rate), the search for national or tribal glory, pre-emptive defence, sheer accident, instructions from God, the urge to 'civilise' others, or simply the innocent curiosity that seems to be a common feature of the human psyche in certain circumstances. There are almost no exceptions, except where a people has found it impossible – often because of rival and stronger imperialisms hedging them in – to expand. Perhaps instead of asking ourselves why certain countries established empires we should ask why certain others *didn't*; and what it was about the circumstances of their times that *enabled* the great empires to be formed.

One general circumstance was the disparities of strength that have always existed between some parts of the world and others, measured and explained not only in terms of military power, but also morally, economically, ideologically, organisationally, geographically, and in terms of what is generally regarded as 'progress' at various times. If the disparity is wide enough it can create vacuums into which the stronger nations are then sucked. This is obvious in the cases of Iberian colonialism in the sixteenth century and northern European in the nineteenth, when, once they decided to take over other countries, the Europeans found they could do it almost effortlessly. Native Americans, north and south, were no match for the superior military technology, and the exotic and fatal diseases, of the colonists and *conquistadores*. This wasn't the case everywhere before the nineteenth century, until which time several non-European empires, notably the Ottoman, Arab, Mughal, Manchu and Asiatic Russian, proved more effective at dominating large parts of the world than the feebler (and divided) Europeans; and disease could work both ways. (It is an arrogant mistake to push the origins of Western global domination much further back than the mid nineteenth century.) Before the nineteenth century there was a great deal of overseas territorial expansion, but fairly limited in its extent and impact, and with many European nations taking part. Britain was certainly not in the lead – if anyone it was Portugal, followed by Spain, the Netherlands and France; and Russia, Austria, China, Turkey and the United States of America, if contiguous empires are included. Much of it met with resistance, and failed. Early on, Britain was as much a victim of it as a perpetrator, at the hands of Romans, Saxons, Vikings and the brutal Norman invasion that is conventionally supposed to have started off its history proper – '1066 and All That'. That's not counting later, friendly takeovers – Stuart, Hanoverian, Chicago School economics – and the imperialistic aggressions Britain fought off – Catholic Spanish, Revolutionary French, Nazi German. In these cases the disparities turned out to be less great than had appeared.

It is worth adding – and relevant to our later discussion – that this sort of thing was not confined to the actions of nations or peoples 'abroad'. Almost exactly the same kinds of disparities existed within every country, for the same reasons – inequalities of various kinds of power – and elicited responses that would have been called 'imperialist' if they *had* happened beyond their frontiers. The English enclosure movement (of the people's land) and the Scottish Highland clearances were both examples of one class of British people 'colonising' another class's territories, in much the same way as happened in north America, Australia and southern Africa. On the other side of the fence, the popular 'allotment' movement of the early twentieth century could be regarded as a working-class attempt to *re*-colonise them back. (In Swedish the word for allotment is '*kolonilott*'.) Other kinds of internal power structure could also be considered to be closely equivalent to imperial ones; enough to suggest to some more politically aware working-class Britons direct comparisons between their own conditions and those of their country's oppressed colonial subjects. A common Radical term to describe factory work was 'wage slavery', clearly with the colonial form of legal slavery in mind. The comparison can be disputed; but it demonstrates that 'imperialism' and 'colonialism' – we shall discuss the semantics of these terms later – were not such special and distinct phenomena as they have often been taken to be. In one form or another, they happened all over and in all ages, between nations and within them, making them one of the constants of human history. (That is not, of course, to justify them. The same could be said of disease.) The British Empire was just one example of many. That should put it in its place. My Swedish friends: mark!

But of course the sort of imperialism the British practised was distinctive – highly so. The main reason for that was the dichotomy that has already been mentioned between its two 'heads'. England's early overseas acquisitions, in France, Ireland and Wales, were gained in an age (the Middle Ages) when the idea of nationality was undeveloped, and had been driven mainly by dynastic – that is, feudal – considerations, and the ideas of military glory and family honour generally associated with them. The motive of plunder was also important, not only to the kings and nobles who participated, but also to the ordinary soldier, as an incentive to put himself in harm's way. In the early twentieth century one prominent Austrian sociologist, unable to conceive of any more rational motive for the imperialism of his own time, thought it must be due to an atavistic social regression to those older aristocratic attitudes.[1] There was a grain of truth in that, as we shall see. But after the Middle Ages the leading motivation changed. Plunder took over; albeit no longer generally called that, which was reasonable in the main. Most of Britain's expansion into the wider world followed new trade routes, and was justified on the grounds that it did not simply plunder places, but exchanged goods with them, fairly, at mutually agreed prices, to the benefit of both sides, without any compulsion on Britain's part, and no transfer of territory, apart from the lease of a few coastal entrepôts. Elsewhere it consisted of the settlement of surplus British people in parts of the world that were thought to be virgin, or at least not greatly cultivated, to farm for themselves – by their own labour, that is – which is the strict meaning of 'colonisation' (from the Latin *colore*, to cultivate; hence the *kolonilott*). Like plunder, its purpose was profit, but equitably achieved. It also introduced capitalism into the picture, with the great British East India Company – chartered by Elizabeth I in 1600 – relying on invested risk capital, essentially. That can be taken to mark the beginning of what today is called 'capitalist imperialism'. But of course this picture of it is an overly rosy one.

From now on the relationship between 'feudal' and 'capitalist' forms of imperialism becomes complicated. (This is another place where the 'two heads' analogy rather breaks down.) A few aristocrats – a pretty flexible bunch in Britain, by contrast with many continental aristocracies, which may be why they didn't get their heads chopped off – went along with capitalism in a big way, so long as it didn't involve getting their hands dirty. They took to foreign trade in particular, and later financial services, because they didn't involve *making* things, in those dreadful northern industrial cities, but could be conducted from comfortable oak-panelled boardrooms made up to look like gentlemen's clubs in the City of London, or simply by mail. This has been called 'gentlemanly capitalism'.[2] Later the links between the aristocracy and the capitalist middle classes were further cemented from the other side when successful capitalists – a few of them – used their wealth to buy themselves into the aristocracy, though the results of that were often to snuff out their entrepreneurial spirit, and *still* leave them looked down on by the genuine – that is, landed, established and often relatively impoverished – aristos. ('His family was in trade, you know!'[3]) But this just illustrates the depth of the gulf that existed between the middle and upper classes in the nineteenth century, which could easily survive a bit of class mobility at the edges.

Meanwhile capitalist imperialism forged ahead. Its success was based largely on Britain's Industrial Revolution – the world's first, of course – partly financed by profits from the East India and other trades, which transformed not only Britain's economy but also her society and, eventually, her politics between, roughly, 1750 and 1850. One common view of this is that the Industrial Revolution produced so much in the way of new products – mainly machines and textiles, exhibited proudly in London's Great Exhibition of 1851 – and paid the workers who manufactured them so little, that Britain *had* to find external markets for them, in lieu of domestic consumption, or the economy would collapse through overproduction. She also desperately needed foreign raw materials – American raw cotton is the leading example – to manufacture many of these items. Another way of looking at it, not necessarily inconsistent with this, is that British industrial production created its own markets abroad, by stimulating demand. Whichever; the process snowballed throughout the later eighteenth and the nineteenth centuries, by what seems to be an internal expansionist dynamic of its own (a common business mantra is that firms must either 'grow or die'), hugely extending Britain's presence, influence and sometimes control ('empire') in almost every part of the world.

According to the dominant ideology of the day – then called 'Political Economy', or free trade – this should have been unproblematic; indeed, the very reverse. But hopes for free-market capitalism then were different in many respects from what they became later. For a start, it was supposed to conduce to greater social *equality*, which seems surprising in the light of twenty-first-century trends; unless the fault now is that it isn't allowed to be free *enough*: all those bank bailouts, and the like. John Stuart Mill, who wrote a major nineteenth-century textbook on Political Economy, needed to believe this, as one of his main justifications for the free market, and indeed stated that if he was ever proved to be wrong about it, he would become 'a communist'.[4] This is basically why free marketists then could still call themselves 'Liberals', without the modern 'New' to qualify it. Secondly – and another reason for the 'Liberal' tag – they believed strongly that free trade was the most powerful *antidote* to imperialism, rather than an agency of it, as it became widely regarded later. For example, Richard Cobden, the great mid-Victorian free-trade activist, believed it would bring an end to 'the desire and the motive for large and mighty empires; [and] for gigantic armies and great navies – for those materials which are used for the destruction of life and the desolation of the rewards of labour'; all this 'as man becomes one family, and freely exchanges the fruits of his labour with his brother man'.[5] (Versions of this still inspired American 'Neo-Cons' in the 1990s and early 2000s.) It is important to be aware of these fundamental differences, lest we assess or (worse) judge nineteenth-century Liberals by the assumptions of today.

The reasons why it didn't always happen like that were multiple and complex. Broadly speaking, however, they derived from those power imbalances that we have already remarked as one of the circumstances that could lead to weaker areas 'sucking in' stronger nations, and which also created temptations for strong-nation capitalists to abuse their positions there. In Britain's case it was an economic and ideological imbalance, rather than a military or political one. A prime early example of its effect was the East India Company, one of the first truly global corporations in history, the longest-lived, and arguably the 'greatest'. When presented with a chaotic political situation in the subcontinent after the weakening of native Maratha rule in the mid eighteenth century, and provoked by France (at that time Britain's main European enemy), it had taken advantage of the situation by formally annexing large tracts of the country, which wasn't in the spirit of free trade at all, exacerbating a terrible famine in Bengal in the 1770s (or at least, doing nothing to relieve it); and it had then become progressively more corrupt, its agents enriching themselves scandalously, until it was 'reformed' in 1773. That was quite apart from its notorious complicity in the Indian opium trade, enforced by two wars with China, whose leaders were trying to suppress the drug habit, which was probably its greatest sin, even in contemporary British eyes. China was another of those 'weak' countries then. The 'Opium Wars' were defended on the grounds that Chinese restrictions on the import of opium offended against the principle of free trade. That could be regarded as the other side of Cobden's great ideal.

The Opium Wars were not the only atrocity (as we would regard them today) perpetrated by the British overseas in the age of empire. Several books have been published in recent years – as part of a new sackcloth-and-ashes trend in British imperial history – cataloguing and describing these in detail, from simple cheating through slavery to wholesale massacres;[6] which make painful reading for any sensitive human being, and even more, probably, for anyone who wants to identify him- or herself as a national descendant of these (mainly) men. (We shall return to this – the question of historical 'identity' – much later.) They are regarded as 'imperial British' offences; and of course they essentially were. It was the British government that had granted the East India Company its privileges, and so was ultimately responsible for what it did with them. But it wasn't directly involved. What it had done, effectively, was to subcontract its responsibilities to a capitalist company, in a move that would be called 'privatisation' later on. This became a common device in the later nineteenth century, when large parts of Africa and the Pacific were 'chartered' to private companies in much the same way. Chartering included not only powers over trade, but the right to administer, tax and rule the local peoples, raise armies (the East India Company had arguably a bigger and better army of its own than did metropolitan Britain at that time), declare wars, and conduct foreign policy with neighbours. Another form of privatisation, often combined with the 'charter' one, was to get settlers in the various colonies – where there were enough of them – to perform the duties that, strictly speaking, the government should have taken care of itself. That included relations with native peoples. That was the way in North America, Australasia and southern Africa. It was called 'self-government', or sometimes 'democracy'; but it did not seem particularly democratic to these countries' *indigènes*. Most 'atrocities' against them committed in the British Empire throughout its modern history were directly ascribable to this. (Not quite all. The British and Indian armies were also responsible for some.)

It was done, of course, in order to save money, with the privateers, rather than the Treasury, now saddled with the costs of running colonies. That fitted in nicely with the liberal ideology of the day, which – as with today's 'New' Liberals – disliked taxation as a burden on enterprise. (Money was best left, as Gladstone is supposed to have said, 'to fructify in the pockets of the people'.[7]) Another motive might have been to enable governments to duck out of their responsibilities. In the later nineteenth century many

Liberals, still professing 'anti-imperialism' (after Cobden), certainly thought that chartering commercial companies to run colonies was consistent with that. A theoretical reason for believing that they would be run more cheaply and even beneficently this way was that if it was in the interests of shareholders to save money, they would refrain from pursuing policies that would provoke the colonised into rebellions that might be difficult and expensive to put down. Unfortunately, it did not always work that way, with the privateers (capitalists and settlers) very often inciting unrest, which they knew would force the British government to intervene to pull their chestnuts out of the fire, for reasons of its own. (We shall come on to those reasons later.) Like modern-day banks, they were 'too big to fail'. So, again, this could be regarded as a failure not of the free market, but of the limits that were imposed on it. Be that as it might, it was private enterprise that was responsible for nearly all the awful things that happened in the British Empire from the eighteenth to the twentieth century, rather than 'imperialism' in any more formal sense.

Well, yes, *but*… Of course it depends what you mean by 'imperialism'. People's understanding of that word has shifted radically over time. In the middle of the nineteenth century it was applied exclusively to the military annexation of territories by (usually) 'emperors', and besmirched by being associated, in the modern age, mainly with Napoleon. (That is certainly what Cobden was thinking of.) Nothing short of that was counted; though it did occur to one commentator as early as 1870 that Britain's 'quasi-territorial domination, under treaties' of some countries, and its 'great superiority of general commerce and the carrying trade everywhere', had acquired for her 'almost an empire, in all but name'.[8] 'Almost', note. It was still important that it wasn't called that. It took nearly another century for economic domination to be widely included in the rubric of 'imperialism', usually as 'informal' or 'free trade empire', where it remains. No one today would want to restrict the scope of British imperialism to merely the areas of the world coloured red on those old maps. Since then the definition has been broadened to cover, for example, 'cultural imperialism' (the spread of Protestant Christianity, Western fashion or, less often, football), 'gender imperialism' (men over women), and even internal imperialism (England's colonisation of Scotland and Wales; though I've not yet seen it extended – which would be perfectly logical – to the middle classes' economic and ideological colonisation of England itself). Of course, these are all perfectly legitimate senses of the word, which has no set definition, but can be used as one wants, within certain limits: so long as one makes one's meaning clear. My own preference – but only because it makes it more serviceable as an analytical *tool* – is for a usage that preserves the root implication of the word, power (*imperium*), however that might be exerted; and *abroad*. So, McDonald's would not be included as an example of 'American imperialism' (we choose to eat their rotten burgers, after all); nor would football (no one forced it on the Brazilians) or enclosure, which was Britain's affair alone. Other forms of 'informal' domination would be counted, however, including economic – big corporations with the bargaining power that comes from size, especially monopolies – and cultural, if a religion, say, were forced on a people. This seems straightforward in principle, although there will of course be marginal cases, depending on how much unfair pressure is reckoned to have been exerted on people to sell to them, or buy from them, or change their ways. These marginal cases, incidentally, may even include some of the red-coloured bits of the map, where the degree of imperial rule could not always be measured by the depth of the colour used. That's where judgement comes in.

All these kinds of domination can be called 'imperialistic', which is not to say, however, that the 'imperial' aspect of them is necessarily the crucial one. Often all 'imperialisms' are lumped together as if they came from the same stable, so that calling them 'imperialism' says all that is needed to be said about them. That is lazy, and not usually very enlightening. Within the genus 'imperialism' there were many different varieties, springing from totally different roots. Surveying the old British Empire as a whole, but in some detail, this is obvious: with almost nothing except the name and their common membership of this strange, amorphous and unwieldy arrangement *called* the British Empire to associate the Australian Gold Coast, for example, with the West African one. We shall be meeting with some of these differences later on. The one we need to highlight here, however, because it bears on the opening proposition of this chapter, is between 'formal' imperialism and 'informal'. What has been described up to now has been 'informal', or economic, or 'privatised' imperialism; the kind that, by and large, originally set the British Empire on its way. That of course is associated with the middle-class, capitalist element of British society in the eighteenth and nineteenth centuries. But then there is the other head of the hybrid to consider, too.

The problem with colonies whose administration was subcontracted out to capitalists or settlers, quite apart from the scandals and atrocities, was that the work of administration didn't really suit the capitalists. Free-market capitalists tended to be essentially anti-government, both in principle – because government was viewed as a drag on enterprise – and personally, because entrepreneurs considered they had better things to do with their time and talents: more profitable, that is. Turning your administrative duties *to* personal profit was generally thought to be intrinsically corrupt, with the old East India Company a notorious example of that. But the further British commerce, trade and settlement spread, the more need there was for *someone* to 'look after', or rule, the countries that had been penetrated by them. This was not always because of the capitalists' or settlers' bad behaviour, though it often was. Even with the best and most benevolent will in the world, introducing European commerce into places like Africa and Asia was likely to be beset with problems that capitalism on its own could not sort out. The polities the merchants traded with might not be friendly or stable: subject to local rebellions, for example; even anarchic ('vacuums' again); using the Europeans in their own power struggles; reneging on contracts; attacking their entrepôts; or simply not *recognising* the principles, typically individual property rights, on which Western commerce and land-purchase were based. Hence the need for an impartial – or at least less financially compromised – ruling cadre. Luckily for the privateers (though they often complained about them), and *possibly* luckily for their new accidental subjects, that cadre existed, in the persons of Britain's own, pre-capitalist ruling class, which had by and large kept the reins of the domestic British state in its hands, and for much the same reason: despite the country's domination in so many ways by the commercial and industrial middle classes, the latter weren't keen on the essentially unproductive work of governing. The upper classes were. They also liked soldiering (or, rather, officering), which could come in handy in colonial situations.

Of course, it was not quite as simple as this. There were some upper-class capitalists, as we have seen, and quite a minority of middle-class ministers, civil servants and colonial governors. One problem with the upper class is to define it; in this context it very often means what should strictly be called the upper middle class, 'beneath' the aristocratic level – the most kosher aristocrats didn't generally get involved in *colonial* governing – but who were involved in professional occupations, rather than commerce. There was also another important category, which we shall come on to later: what I call the 'interstitials', who found themselves living in the narrow gaps *between* the conventional social classes, often uncomfortably. Another compromising factor is that in the second half of the nineteenth century most of them came to accept (albeit unenthusiastically) the major middle-class dogma of the time, free trade, which was why the manufacturing and commercial middle classes were happy for them to govern on their behalf. (Palmerston had been taught 'Political Economy' at university.[9]) That was part of their status- and possibly life-saving flexibility. But they retained other upper-class prejudices. Anti-commercialism was one. On the more positive side, they clung to notions of paternalism and *noblesse oblige* – serving others, looking after their peasants, honesty – which fitted them rather better for this new imperial role being asked of them than the cold 'cash nexus' values that Thomas Carlyle (a Tory himself) so despised in the lower middle classes.[10] They also put more emphasis on 'status' than did other classes; not only their own but their nation's in the world, which may have made them more amenable to ideas of British military and imperial prestige. All these values were inculcated in their 'public' schools – Britain's 'peculiar institution' – which, after a period of decline, flourished again from the 1860s onwards, recruiting many middle-middle-class boys (and a few girls) to turn them into upper-middles; just in time – though of course this wasn't an accident – for them to fill the vacancies that were beginning to open up for them in a growing British government service, especially in the colonies. Most colonial civil servants from that time on were recruited from the public schools.

This was the 'head' that spoke for the other side of British imperialism; limiting or modifying the commercial side where it could, and adding a whole raft of colonial ideas and practices which capitalism could never have produced on its own. Public-school-educated colonial agents and officers generally (though generalisations are risky here) took seriously their protective, or paternalistic, function, and also an educative function if they were given the tools. They prided themselves on their integrity. With old-fashioned ideas about class and hierarchy, they tended to respect traditional native kings, princes, emirs, maharajahs, chiefs and the like,[11] which had a bearing on the way they saw their colonies developing in the future. They were more often than not wary of Christian missionaries, for the social disruption they could cause and some of the dangerous ideas they might put into the minds of their converts. They themselves were often quite tolerant of native practices that seemed barbaric to the latter. (Some of them they quite liked.) They defended natives who they thought were being exploited by corporations and settlers; in colonial North America, for example, where one of the (secondary) sparks of the War of Independence was the British government's attempt to put a stop to westward expansion, and the suffering to Native Americans that it was bound to bring in its train. (That wasn't only for humanitarian reasons; they also feared the cost of the British troops that would be necessary to put the 'Indian wars' down.[12]) They were unsuccessful there, of course, and in many other similar instances. Sometimes their protests seem like crocodile tears. But the capitalist leviathan was an immensely powerful engine, and may have been ultimately irresistible, as it seems today.

As well as this, there were certainly downsides to the public-school imperial approach, even where it worked: with paternalism easily turning to patronisation, for example; some insufferable prejudices; a tendency to stasis – for an easy life; and a closed system of loyalty, honour and group secrecy, rendering colonial government often impervious to democratic scrutiny. Some colonial civil servants were corruptible, and many gave in to disillusion towards the ends of their spells abroad. Their integration back into the domestic British professional workforce after decolonisation, for example, was not always successful. (Ex-colonial governors were not what British industry needed.) They preened themselves a lot (called 'ornamentalism'[13]). In fact they had all the vices, as well as the virtues, of the old British gentry class. But they were very different vices from those of the imperial monster's other head. And they did help temper the latter, to an extent. That is the point, if we wish to understand the contradictions of British imperialism.

They may also help explain why outright opposition to imperialism was not so widespread in Britain during the nineteenth century as it became later. Actually, that may be misleading. Anti-imperialism is not the only alternative to imperialism (as a sentiment); other possibilities are apathy, and denial. The earlier nineteenth century was full of both: apathy because only a minority of the population was more than very vaguely aware of what its country got up to overseas (we shall return to this); and denial because, firstly, people did not want to think that Britain could be 'Napoleonic', and secondly because – as we have seen – there was no way they could conceive of free trade as 'imperialistic'. Another factor is that a second alternative to imperialism, as a policy this time, is 'nationalism', and the idea of self-governing nations was a very infant one then. This is because hardly anyone *was* self-governing, in this age before democracy (the main exception was the USA, and even there it was restricted to white males), when nearly everyone except for the rulers was ruled by the latter, whether they were stationed abroad or at home. Most political debates centred around whether they were ruled *fairly*, which not everyone – the exceptions in Britain were the Chartists – assumed could only be done by themselves. Even most European countries at that time were either parts of empires, like the Austro-Hungarian, Russian or Ottoman, or messes of little statelets, like Germany. Britain was lucky in having natural boundaries which fused it as a nation (or at least an independent country) before most others; but even Britain resisted extending this logic to its sister island of Ireland until late on. So the notion of 'independence' did not carry the same resonance it does today. Added to which was the consideration that national independence in some parts of the world seemed highly unlikely to furnish the benefits that became blithely associated with it later: if countries were too 'backward' or 'primitive', as the expressions went then; vulnerable, for example, to marauding slave traders, or even marauding capitalists; or threatening the stability of more settled neighbours. There were people in Britain in the nineteenth century whose instincts were undoubtedly what we would call 'anti-imperialist'. Cobden was one. He thought the market would solve the problem, naturally. But what if you didn't have that naive confidence? In this case withdrawing from your colonies could simply leave their inhabitants to worse fates. That was undoubtedly insincere in some cases – a mere pretext – but it was neither an illiberal nor an unreasonable argument. The recent collapses of the Yugoslav (Serbian) and Soviet empires *may* – it's too early to tell as yet – bear that out.

Another reason for the weakness of overt anti-imperialism at this time was that there was no great political movement to take it up. Until quite late in the nineteenth century the only mainstream choice one had in British politics was between the new shiny radicalism of the free-market Liberals (promising greater equality ultimately, remember), and the backward-looking protectionism and paternalism of the Tories. (You couldn't vote Chartist. Indeed, that was their grouse.) For those who disputed the claims of Liberalism to make everything better for everyone Toryism seemed the only alternative. Carlyle was a Tory; so was Charles Dickens, one of the early nineteenth century's greatest propagandists for social reform, and a firm non-believer in the Liberal utopia. Dickens was also a racist, which was his reason for not supporting humanitarian imperialism – other races weren't worth it – but we'll come on to that later. If you weren't racist, however, and wanted to protect other peoples from the depredations of capitalist imperialism, you had to be a Tory, or sympathetic to them. Later, when socialism took more of a hold, it was often in closer league with this kind of Tory than with free marketists. The political consensus of 1945–79, before Thatcher 'dried out' (her expression) the old Tory party – marginalising the paternalists in favour of the 'cash-nexus' brigade – was built on this socialist–paternalist alliance. (Clement Attlee is the key figure here: leader of the Labour party, and founder of Britain's welfare state, but coming from the most 'imperialistic' public school in the country.) Before that, the British Empire even had a number of professed socialists running it. (Sydney – later Lord – Olivier is the leading example.) At the turn of the twentieth century, socialist imperialism along these lines was fairly common: based on the idea, not of abolishing the Empire, but turning it into a socialist commonwealth. George Bernard Shaw wrote a characteristically impish pamphlet on this.[14] These people may have been deluded, and today, of course, are usually dismissed as *echt* imperialists in sheep's clothing, rather than vice versa. But it is easy to see how attractive this kind of alternative was to those who, in genuine anti-imperialist fashion, hugely disapproved of the effects of the more materialist kind of imperialism, yet felt they could not, in justice to its victims, simply wash their hands.

This may help explain why the imperial monster's two heads were fiercer than its tail (as one might expect from the analogy); and also constantly snapping at one another's throats, right to the end. At the root of Britain's imperial expansion in the eighteenth, nineteenth and twentieth centuries, as has long been acknowledged, were its great industrial and capitalist revolutions; *but* with the resistance to those revolutions, and the values associated with them, being almost as significant as capitalism itself. The Empire was carved out by one sort of imperialist, but ruled, where it was effectively ruled at all, by another. We mustn't apply this dichotomy too strictly. There were exceptions, plenty of compromises, and places where it simply doesn't apply.

It is only meant to indicate different approaches to imperialism, in order to make some sense of its fundamental
contradictions; and also to show how it related to Britain's
domestic situation, of 'hybridity'. Without understanding
that, we can't hope to get to grips with the complex nature
of the phenomenon; more complex, admittedly, and as the
following chapters will try to show, than this simple, binary
analysis might suggest.

TWO

Riding the Beast

A T THE ROOT of Britain's expansion in the world in modern times was pretty obviously simple economics, in particular trade early on and then finance, fuelled by her industrial and capitalist revolutions, but tempered, when it came to ruling colonies, by this pre-capitalist survival. On top of this basic dynamic, however, were other factors. Once on its feet and running, the beast was mounted by groups of people with other ideas, interests and motivations that happened to point in the same direction. Among them were politicians, do-gooders and national glory hunters. Sometimes they thought that the British Empire was their doing. It wasn't; but they could make a difference to it.

Politicians got involved mainly because they were called on to protect the interests of British trade against challenges from other poli*ties*. In most cases, only they had the means to do this, especially soldiers to enforce the capitalists' or settlers' rights, and diplomats to negotiate them. In principle the British Foreign Office was not terribly keen on this: the general rule was that if private Englishmen sought great profits in dangerous places, they had to accept the risks that came with that and pay for any associated costs privately, rather than burdening the British Treasury with the expense;[1] but it frequently found itself flouting that general liberal principle, for reasons of its own – or rather, for broader national reasons that it was in a particular position to perceive. One was to do with global commerce. Britain was always vulnerable to having access to her markets, or potential markets, cut off by other countries, which would have done more harm to her than it would to countries less reliant on overseas trade. She had two preferred policies for preventing this. One was to maintain a navy large enough to 'rule the waves' – and therefore the routes between her and her markets. The other was free-trade agreements, by which other nations promised *not* to obstruct her trade. It was Richard Cobden who negotiated the first of these, with France in the 1860s, named 'the Cobden Treaties' as a result; but his ambition went further: to cover the whole world with such arrangements, which was his ultimate solution, as we have seen, to the problems both of 'imperialism', and of large military and naval expenditure. In the meantime, however, British interests had to be protected as and when they came under threat. The 'Opium Wars' with China, conducted on the pretext of forcing the Chinese to honour a free-trade pact with Britain, were an example; but they were not the only one. Most of the others were less unsavoury, but could cost (native) lives, and in any case appeared bullying and arrogant. The most notorious was probably the 'Don Pacifico' incident of 1850. (Greece was threatened with retaliatory action unless she compensated a Gibraltarian merchant attacked by a mob in Athens.) Under Palmerston this became known as 'gunboat diplomacy'.

The 'bullying' was because the foes Palmerston directed his gunboats' fire at nearly always appeared very much weaker militarily than Britain, and so soft targets, in a way. That didn't, incidentally, prevent the occasional rebuff, especially on land, from 'native' armies that proved smarter than and at least as brave as the British, resulting in a number of quite startling humiliations at the hands of Zulus, Maoris, Afghans (repeatedly), Indian 'mutineers', Sudanese jihadists and ill-armed 'Boers' (South Africans of Dutch origin) among others; which underlined Britain's own military weakness once she disembarked from the security of her ships. It was largely for this reason that the British Foreign and War Offices studiously avoided becoming entangled in any of Europe's continental wars for nearly a century after 1815, with the sole exception of the Crimean War, Britain's experience of which (she would never have won the war on her own) was enough to convince them of the wisdom of this general policy, later rather flattered by being given the name of 'splendid isolation'. The continental European powers, of course, were a completely different kettle of sharks from Britain's extra-European enemies, three or four of them having far larger and fiercer armies than she did. Isolation from them, however, could only be achieved if none of them attacked *her*; which the Navy ('wooden walls') *might* be able to protect her from, and the Continent's political disarray in the earlier nineteenth century – still in the process of 'unifying' – made unlikely; but not for long. Britain's strategy then, rather than creating an army on a continental scale, which the dominant liberal dogma of the time thought would be counter-productive – it would require higher taxes, and taking men out of productive work, so undermining the economy that would be expected to support it; obviously the other, older 'head' of the monster didn't altogether go along with that – was to seek, by negotiation, to maintain what it called a 'Balance of Power' in Europe, between four or five of the 'Great Powers', shored up with mutual treaties of defence, ensuring that if one did aggress the others would gang up together to rein it back; including Britain, but with the guarantee of better-armed allies on her side. (This was different, incidentally, from the *bi*-lateral 'balance' that is familiar to us from Cold War times.) This was one of the reasons why Britain was no great supporter of nationalist movements on the Continent, in the Habsburg Empire, for example (Italy, Hungary), for fear that they could weaken one of these essential 'balancing' weights. (Although, always being realists, the British Foreign Office could easily swap sides when it appeared the nationalists were winning.) This must undermine Britain's reputation in some circles, both then and now, for being a 'Great Power' in the 'powerful' sense of the word. If she was, it was because she chose her enemies carefully.

Of course Britain turned this into a virtue (just as Swedes I know turn their nation's 'neutrality' in World

War II). Her liberals' argument was that she had progressed beyond the stage of human social development which prized territorial conquest and military glory, but in which the Continent still appeared entrapped, until hopefully the light of free trade would spread and teach it how trivial and simply not worth fighting over these matters were. In the meantime her national interest in trade – not at all trivial – turned her attention to the wider world, where she did most of it (roughly 65 per cent in 1860, for example, as against France's 35 per cent and Belgium's 15 per cent[2]), and in which, luckily, her powerful European rivals were less interested, and local rivals weaker. That is where most of Britain's wars took place in the nineteenth century, almost continuously; often called her 'little wars' today, but they were not at all little, of course, to the locals who were gunned down. (As Hilaire Belloc famously and poetically put it: 'Whatever happens, we have got / The Maxim gun, and they have not.'[3]) Native casualties often weren't counted, in either sense of the word. The politicians also presented such engagements as 'defensive', but 'defence' and 'aggression', in these circumstances of great inequality between the sides, are in the eye of the beholder. If a war was defensive, it could be presented as a police operation. More crucially, they were usually *cheap*, and so managed to pass well under the radar of the House of Commons, which – being middle-class dominated – was mainly interested in things that cost taxpayers' money. (Plus religion; and certain humanitarian causes.) Foreign policy in distant parts of the world generally didn't cost, until it threatened to lead to more major involvements, like the Indian, Maori and South African wars. Those *were* debated. The minor ones, however, were very often not even reported back home. Which is one of the things that gave the Victorians the extraordinary illusion that they were a peaceful – even pacifist – people, living in accordance with the Christian Gospel they so ardently professed.

The end result of many of these wars, even when it had not been originally intended, was the annexation of territory, extending the area of the formal British Empire thereby. In these cases annexation was the only way markets – or in some cases the routes to markets: this was the key to the (virtual) annexation of Egypt (lying across the Suez Canal) and of much of East Africa in the 1880s and 1890s – could be secured; not only for Britain, but, under the rules of free trade, for every other commercial nation, which was supposed to make it all right. (When the Victorians thought of 'imperialism' or 'colonialism', they usually saw it in mercantilist terms. Anything short of a colonial monopoly didn't properly count.) It is worth making the point, however, that colonies weren't always taken by military force, but could be negotiated or traded into Britain's hands, or even offered to her voluntarily ('empire by invitation'[4]). And by the later eighteenth century, of course, Britain already had a number, inherited from way back. Nevertheless, however the eggs arrived in the nest, the task of hatching them was then handed over from the Foreign and War Offices to the Colonial or India Offices. That's when their work, and that of their upper-class paternalistic servants, began.

The Colonial Office was regarded as a quite lowly Department of State until the very end of the nineteenth century, possibly reflecting the domestic status of the Empire generally. The India Office, which took over the government of India from the East India Company after the disastrous 'Mutiny' of 1857–8, had far more esteem, deriving probably from the spectacular nature of the Indian colony, which in fact was never *called* a 'colony', but always 'an Empire', quite apart from the broader British one. When Disraeli made Queen Victoria an 'Empress' in 1876, it was of India alone. India's British rulers, too, were a cadre of their own: quite in-bred; originally inherited from the old Company set-up, but purified now from their old corruption; socially distinct even from their own upper-middle class in Britain; with their own public school (Haileybury and Imperial Service College: Attlee's); reputedly much brighter than their Colonial equivalents – they had to take a stiff exam to join the Service; and with their own army (Indian 'sepoys' officered by Europeans) even after the Company one had been dissolved. Many of them identified with 'their' India more than they did with Britain, and stayed on after independence. There was very little exchange of personnel between India and the 'lesser' colonies. At the end of the nineteenth century the ultra-imperialist Colonial Secretary Joseph Chamberlain tried to boost the kudos of the latter, with some success. But the two administrations need to be discussed separately.

Britain's Indian Empire was an autocracy, though one that couldn't be autocratised too much. This was because the 'red line' of British rulers was very thin there: around

2,000 civil servants (plus British officers of the Indian Army) in a population of 270 million – this is in 1900; which meant that they had to collaborate with the locals, or with sections of them (sometimes called 'divide and rule'), in order to maintain their authority at all. Often this numerical weakness is forgotten, with the result that the British hold on India is assumed to have been tighter than it was. The same was true of most of Britain's other colonies, although in some of those she had her settlers to help her out. In parts of India – the 'Princely States' of (mainly) the interior – power was devolved instead to traditional rulers, who governed almost as they liked under British 'protection'. In the bits she ruled directly, the British first tried to get along as well as they could with the native Indians, sometimes becoming quite 'Indianised' themselves (taking Indian mistresses and wives, for example); then in the very early nineteenth century trying – some of them – to 'civilise' the Indians, chiefly by preaching Christianity and Lockean principles of land ownership to them, and weaning them away from what they regarded as 'savage' superstitions and customs. (That is, more 'superstitious' than the idea of the Resurrection. That's the little barb that got me into trouble with that American schools board.) For many British in India at that time this was seen, probably genuinely, as a way of 'improving' the country to the level from which she could start ruling herself. Eventually. That idea suffered a mortal blow, however, when the ungrateful Indians rebelled against their rulers in 1857, in a bloody war that took most of the puff out of the reformers' sails. Thereafter the policy was to tolerate Indian customs and practices roughly as they were (exceptions were made in cases of *sati* and *thuggee* – widow-immolation and religious murder); out of despair, for an easy life, or occasionally because individual Britons had come to appreciate them; and to confine their 'improvements' to material and technical things, like building railways. Britain, after all, was undeniably good at that.

The Indian government also ran a few colonies outside the subcontinent, in the Persian Gulf, for example; but most of the others came under the Colonial Office, in a variety of shapes and sizes. British policies varied enormously according to their types. One was the 'settlement' (sometimes 'white settlement') colonies, especially British North America (later Canada), Australia, New Zealand and South Africa, which were always largely self-governing (the whites, that is), and early on were widely assumed to be bound to go the way of the United States soon. In 1812 the United States tried to anticipate this, by invading British North America, but then found the Canadians wanted nothing to do with them. (This is sometimes miscalled the United States' 'Second War of Independence'. If anything it was the Canadians'.) Most British politicians were quite relaxed about this. Upper-class ones would have been quite happy to see those awful democratic places go. (They were giving the plebs at home ideas.) So far as the Colonial Office was concerned, its main tasks with regard to Canada were to try to sort out the ethnic conflict between the British and French, and negotiate trade deals with other countries, including the metropole. It was supposed to protect the 'aboriginals' also, but rather failed in this – as it did in Australia too. It didn't do much actual ruling. Canada remained wary of being swallowed up by its southern neighbour, against which British imperial support was vital. In the later nineteenth century great imperialistic schemes were floated for unifying all the 'white' colonies with Britain in a worldwide federation, which could then compete properly with the really 'great' – that is, large and populous – powers in trade and everything else. Australasia and South Africa were to be included in this too. But little came of it; and the 'white' empire, later 'Commonwealth', staggered along in a fairly friendly way, acquiring more and more local independence, until being implicitly spurned by Britain when she joined the European Common Market (later European Union) in 1973.

Other colonial responsibilities didn't have the settlement colonies' advantages – from the Colonial Office's point of view, that is. From that of the original populations it was almost always disastrous to live in a white settlement colony, with government over you, as well as over everything else, devolved to these incomers whose main interest in being amongst you was to get your lands and labour cheap. (The scanty remains of the original Tasmanians – almost completely wiped out in one way or another in thirty years – attest to that.) In the non-settlement colonies it could be different. There were no settlers there to delegate to, or they were too few to run things themselves. There were some marginal ones: majority African countries which settlers tried controlling but ultimately proved too few to succeed – Kenya, the Rhodesias and South Africa in the very long run. Most of the rest were packed full of *indigènes*, with cultures of their own, and the potential always, because of their numbers, to pull the rug from under you. These were the stamping grounds of your stereotypical Colonial Governor and District Officer: in full dress (in stifling climates), big hats with ostrich feathers, pith helmets and khaki shorts for his underlings, gin and tonics at sundown (the tonic good for the malaria), ruling over palm and pine, and retiring quite young – because it took a lot out of you – to Cheltenham or Tunbridge Wells, or perhaps to become a university registrar.[5]

Generally they were expected just to hold their forts. That meant making sure their colonies were defended against foreign predators and internal ne'er-do-wells; safe to conduct business in, and to preach in, although Colonial officers tended to distrust missionaries (at any rate the subversive rather than the 'give unto Caesar' type); dispensing justice in a rough and ready, and part-indigenous, kind of way; balancing their budgets: almost the fundamental principle of British colonial rule everywhere was that it should be 'self-sufficing', that is, financed from local taxes, on either the merchants or the natives; and – really – very little else. In other words, it was mainly an administrative job. If they succeeded in this, and in not stirring up their natives too much, they were regarded as successful, and allowed to retire with honours (CBEs, and so on). From about the end of the nineteenth century more became expected of them: to positively 'improve' or develop their colonial wards, in order to justify their hold on them in a period when colonialism was becoming more competitive, and controversial, as we shall see. That could prove difficult.

Because colonial governors only very rarely came from the commercial middle classes, and had been taught to 'serve' (at the good old 'public' schools), they weren't generally the enthusiastic friends of capitalists, one obvious agent of 'development', who tended to resent them, as businessmen usually do with governments. This was often the complaint in India, for example, although in view of the extent of the commercial exploitation that went on there it seems unreasonable. In West Africa at the turn of the twentieth century, shocked by the revelations of gruesome atrocities committed in 'King Leopold's Congo' (it was that bad old king's personal fiefdom), by private companies granted 'concessions' to farm rubber there, the Colonial Office inaugurated a policy designed expressly to prevent that kind of system in its own West African colonies, to the annoyance (to put it mildly) of the Liverpool soap firm of Lever Brothers, which had wanted to introduce large-scale plantations of nut-bearing palm trees (for 'Palmolive' soap) to Nigeria.[6] That was a clear pre-capitalist paternalist reaction; especially as the Colonial Office's alternative way of 'developing' Nigeria (just conserving was no longer acceptable) was by confirming the peasants in the ownership of their lands. The argument was that people work better for themselves than as capitalist 'wage slaves'. The upper classes had always tried to look after their peasants. (To be fair, there are not many other examples, though there are some.)

The best example may be Britain's assault on one particular sort of trade, and a particular sort of private property, in the early nineteenth century, when she succeeded in abolishing her own slave trade between the West Indies and Africa (1807); enacting laws that would enable her to intercept other countries' slave ships; and then abolishing the institution of slavery itself throughout the whole of her empire (1833) – that is, in the Afrikaner (Dutch-origin) parts of South Africa as well. It was an impressive achievement, although the slave-owners were generously compensated for the loss of their human property; the argument has been made that slave-produced sugar was becoming uneconomic anyway; the practice did survive elsewhere in other forms; and the effect of abolition on the liberated slaves was merely to throw them on the mercy of the market, which could be more cruel than *some* forms of slavery (where you had 'good' owners). The other downside is that the Victorians made an awful lot of it later, preening themselves on it, and repeatedly citing it as a main feature of their enlightened colonial policy, so that it rather over-shadowed the rest. Both then and in very recent times – for example, history as taught in schools under the national curriculum – the Slavery Abolition Act is singled out and lauded, without mentioning that the slavery it abolished was a British imperial thing too. *Or* a private enterprise thing; depending on how we want to look at it.

Humanitarianism, in fact, was another of those motives 'riding' our monster, and sometimes claiming to drive it. Some religious people maintained that God had given Britain her empire in order to improve the lot of her people, which for them, of course, meant bringing them to Christ. The very early nineteenth century was a highly evangelical time, with most of the great British missionary societies having been founded in the fifty years before, and hundreds of preachers of the One True Word either following the flag, or beating out the path for it. But there were also secular versions of this. They were rooted in Britain's obvious superiority to other countries in most ways; obvious, that is, if you were the usual narrow-minded Brit travelling almost anywhere abroad for the first time in the nineteenth century. It needs to be emphasised at this point, because it becomes relevant later, that this prejudice was by no means universal in Britain, with many people despairing of – for example – the decline in her manners, the squalor of her new industrial cities, the blandness of her food, and a score of other things, and some of them actually preferring the cultures and institutions of foreign countries. Nearly everyone acknowledged that Britain was near the bottom of the European league when it came to the fine arts, for example, and a few even put her lower than India. One of the British people's most consistent national characteristics has been self-denigration. England? 'There the men are as mad as he', says a character in *Hamlet*. But Shakespeare probably didn't mean that. And for others the fact that the British were poor at painting and music and the rest (after Shakespeare's time, at any rate) was not necessarily that shameful. That is why the British bits of the Great Exhibition (about half of it) concentrated on her manufactures. All the pretty stuff was to be found in the French, Italian and Indian galleries. Some Britons even prided themselves on their national philistinism. It was one of the things that boosted their superiority in other ways.

Being at a stage of national development where they no longer had to waste their time, effort and capital on such marginal and aristocratic pursuits, they could concentrate on what really mattered: which was making useful things, and money.[7]

That was how 'progress' was widely defined in nineteenth-century Britain. Her superiority could be measured by material wealth achieved through hard work and enterprise, supplemented by honesty, and the other virtues that honest-to-goodness Protestant Christianity conferred. No amount of art could compete with that. These were the ways in which the rest of the world, again 'obviously', was inferior to Britain; including her European neighbours, who were the 'others' (to use a post-colonial expression, usually applied to non-Europeans) she most often measured herself against. That said, it seemed only neighbourly to confer these benefits on the poor benighted others. If the Victorians were right about 'progress', they would come to them anyway. Britain was swimming with the current, ahead of everyone else. She could show the way. And of course it helped that 'civilised' peoples would make better customers for her trade. David Livingstone's famous partnering of 'commerce and Christianity' as the key to Britain's mission in 'darkest' Africa is often taken as evidence of the true capitalist nature of missionary work, but that may be unfair. Livingstone himself saw it the other way around. By fostering honest trade – that is, replacing the horrendous slave trade – on the west coast of Africa, you were helping to 'raise' its people. So free exchange was a means to 'civilisation'; possibly the only necessary one. That of course was a very mid-nineteenth-century liberal view. It all seemed quite easy.

But in fact it turned out not to be; and towards the end of the nineteenth century the 'civilising mission', if you still believed in it – and it was necessary to pretend to, at least, in order to justify your rule over 'backward' peoples – was coming to require much more. In Britain's case there had nearly always been an element of 'trusteeship' threading through her colonial policy, based on the idea that she was exercising a positive 'trust' for the natives, akin to the position of an adult over a minor, to prepare them for the point when (to mix metaphors) they would fly the nest. It was the 'preparation' that was the key. There were disagreements about how to do this. Education was almost universally agreed to be essential; but what kind? Lord Macaulay is notorious in British imperial history for wanting the Indians to be schooled in British history and literature exclusively: there was nothing of worth in Indian cultures, he believed;[8] and I have Australian friends who complain to this day that just about the only history they got in their schools was the Tudors and Stuarts. (I've pointed out to them that it wasn't 'our' fault. It was the Australian education authorities that insisted on this; possibly because of the need *they* felt to emphasise their British links. Look at the Australian flag.) Western medicine had an even stronger claim to be taught to colonial subjects unsullied, because it was scientific and 'empirical', unlike 'traditional' medicines – 'witch doctors', and the like. The same applied to British forms of government, which were – again – believed to be suited to anyone anywhere. In fact very little of this last was introduced to the 'natives' until very late on in their colonial story, possibly because the British never genuinely considered self-government for them, or because they believed they still had plenty of time to 'develop' them: a century, at least. (It had taken the English a thousand years, from the Danes to democracy, after all.) Before then, however, a new generation of British colonial rulers was beginning to reject many of the chauvinistic assumptions that lay behind the whole project of 'Westernisation'; with regard not only to economics, but also education, government and even the human sciences. Some of the implications of this will be explored in a later chapter. For the moment, however, the point needs to be made that the 'civilising mission' could be controversial.

The idea of it stuck to British imperialism, however, throughout its history; even surviving it after the empire *qua* empire was gone. 'Liberal imperialism' was invented (or at least first called that) around the turn of the twentieth century, in response to criticism of the non-liberal sort, to be revived again at the turn of the twenty-first, albeit under the new name of 'liberal interventionism'. (The Americans in particular felt uncomfortable with the other 'i'-word.) It was (and is) supposed to be the antithesis of, or at least a softer alternative to, 'imperialism' of the red-in-tooth-and-claw variety. The idea is that the enormous problems of the world, which of course are genuine – starvation, genocides, 'failed states', civil war, ignorance, human trafficking, capitalist exploitation (if you don't see that as a solution), more recently 'terrorism' – cannot be solved except through the intervention in its affairs by more 'advanced', fortunate and benevolent countries. Recently this has usually been military, and spearheaded by the United States. It is undoubtedly a worthier motive for 'imperialism', or whatever we like to call it, than many others. Whether it has ever been an originating motive, however – a 'cause' – must be open to some doubt; especially in the light of the fact that most 'humanitarian interventions' (not all) have taken place where there are also more material benefits to be sought, like gold, or rubber, or land, or human cattle (slaves), or oil.

The other problem with 'liberal imperialism', of course, is the solid and burning contradiction that lies at its core. How can you force 'freedom' on people? In the end this was one of the things that undid the British Empire, as we shall see.

Among all the riders of our monster, 'imperialists' undoubtedly came last. By 'imperialists' in this context is meant men and women who identified themselves as such, had imperial ideologies and agendas, and deliberately set out to build an empire per se. There used to be a version of British imperial history that attributed it all to these individuals, great men (usually) who early on had visions of Britain ruling the world, or at least a lot more of it (Millais's famous 1871 painting of *The Boyhood of Raleigh* encapsulates this), and then (like the grown-up Raleigh) went out and pushed the project on. The great (and first) British imperial historian, J. R. Seeley, was keen on this view, and regretted that so few of his compatriots gave these heroes the credit they deserved. Partly of course this is a matter of historical philosophy and approach: depending on what emphasis you give *generally* to the role of individuals in history, as opposed, say, to more impersonal trends and imperatives; or, in this context, to Raleigh's motives and deeds, by comparison with the rise of the Elizabethan state or the expansion of its economy. (Or even the grace of God.) This is not the place to discuss that.

Three things we can say, however. They are, firstly, that this view of the 'Making of the Empire' is a comparatively late one, hardly predating Millais's picture, and only really popular, through boys' books and so on, from the 1890s onwards. Second, that the very idea of the British 'Empire', in this form, is also quite late, with those red-painted world maps, for example, not really appearing on the scene until the 1900s; before then the phrase was used, but could denote many things.[9] And lastly, that we don't really find anyone in Britain taking a particular national pride in the Empire, or pressing for its expansion as such – that is, apart from advocating little incursions in particular parts of the world – before Seeley himself. The few writers and politicians who realised that this was becoming a world-wide phenomenon – Charles Dilke is an example – weren't particularly assertive about it, and in any case generally confined their attention to just one form of imperialism: typically the settlement colonies, or (not *and*) India. (Seeley, for example, was surprisingly dismissive of India.) There was no recognisably imperialist party or other political group-ing before possibly 1870 (though Disraeli's adoption of the cause for the Conservatives then was somewhat superficial), or, more reliably, the 1890s, under the leadership of Joseph Chamberlain in the Unionist party and Lord Rosebery of the Liberal Imperialists, or 'Lib-Imps'. It was then that we find a significant number of politicians and others having the augmentation, safeguarding and unity of the Empire as a major policy. (We shall come on to their ideologies in a later chapter.) But that came long after the Empire was formed, and not far off when it reached its greatest extent; so it can have had little to do with driving the beast. Empire came before imperialism. And, for that reason, long before 'anti-imperialism' too.

That, hopefully, has placed or situated the main factors – two heads and a couple of riders up – that were responsible for the growth of the British Empire and the way it was governed. The following chapters will elaborate on some of this: imperial philosophy, anti-imperial philosophy, the kinds of people who ran the Empire, empire and 'race', and the domestic social and cultural context and impact of imperialism and the Empire; before coming on to the decline and fall of the Empire (starting around 1850, in my idiosyncratic view, but not entirely done with yet), and its effects on – just about everything.

THREE

Imperialisms, Left and Right

FOR THOSE WHO DID embrace imperialism, consciously that is – you could have imperialist attitudes without realising it – it could be an exhilarating ride. To have a part in the 'greatest empire ever' (a quarter of the world, or whatever) was an enormous source of national pride for those who preened themselves on such things as accidental allegiances – most of them had done little *themselves* to be proud of in this regard – and a cause for celebration. 'Jingoism' – raucous demonstrations of national patriotism – was one way this could be expressed. (The word comes from a tub-thumping music-hall song of 1878.) At that level, of course, it was merely visceral, and usually very vague. ('My dad's bigger than your dad.') We shall be returning to it in a couple of chapters. More 'thinking' imperialists often deplored it, as just another manifestation of hooliganism, unlikely to further the imperialist cause in any constructive way. For them there was much more to imperialism than that; and much more, too, than the underlying commercial basis of it, which the more idealistic imperialists considered demeaning.

In this connection it seems extraordinary now that there was a time, fairly recently, when imperialists used to question the underlying capitalist dynamic of imperialism, and to denounce those of us who asserted it as being 'Marxists'. That was in the years before the great counter-revolution of 1979 (in Britain), when red-in-tooth-and-claw capitalism appeared to have been seen off by the more 'progressive' spirit of the age, represented by welfare socialism and the like; with the result that even Conservative politicians were reluctant to espouse it openly, or at least not by that name (another 'c'-word). In those days the main intellectual battles over the ex-Empire were between those who saw it in material terms – usually anti-imperialists – and those whose opinion of it was more 'elevated'. Then came the shock rehabilitation of capitalism, represented in Britain by Margaret Thatcher. Shortly afterwards, even right-wing histories of the Empire seemed happy relating it to commerce. The fact, however, that the capitalist view of imperialism has now won (for the moment?) should not blind us to the fact that British imperialism, in common probably with most other modern imperialisms, did have an idealistic side too. This was essential to its appeal, in a country whose people liked to regard themselves as 'better' than others, and not only at making profits.

The model that British imperialists took for themselves was, of course, the ancient Roman Empire; 'of course' because it was the only one of the great historical empires that Britain (or most of her) had ever been a part of; and because it featured so prominently in the education of her elite. Public-school syllabuses were famously centred firmly on what were called the 'Classics' – if a boy could master these he could do anything – with the result that most upper- and middle-class young men knew far more about ancient Roman and Greek history than they did of their own country's, and, by extension, more about the Roman Empire than about the British. That was scarcely ever taught. Once people realised, fairly late in the nineteenth century, that Britain, too, was accumulating an 'empire', comparisons proliferated. Generally they were proud ones. (Palmerston – from his Roman-looking villa in Hampshire – famously used one when he was browbeating the Greeks over the Don Pacifico affair in 1850; just as the Romans had, he claimed, British travellers abroad should need simply to say the words '*civis Britannicus sum*' in order to put the fear of intervention by the British '*imperium*' in the minds of their foreign persecutors.) Rome was the inescapable precedent. Its great selling point was that it was supposed to have been the means of bringing 'civilisation' to more backward regions of the ancient world, including the country of the Angles. Wasn't modern Britain, the New Rome, doing exactly the same today?

There were, however, problems with that. Rome was not a very attractive comparison otherwise: grand and mighty, yes, but most Classical scholars preferred the grace, intelligence and (supposed) democracy of ancient Greece. (This may have been in the mind of the classically trained Harold Macmillan when he once suggested to President Kennedy that the USA was like Rome to Britain's Greece.[1]) There was also no denying the extreme cruelty of the Romans, meted out to plenty of British tribes under their occupation, provoking serious revolts that are fairly well known, but perhaps less so than they would be if all the accounts of them had not been by Roman scribes. If the Catuvellauni and Iceni had had their own literatures, for example, we might have had fuller and more sympathetic pictures of Caractacus and Boudicca, two of their rebellious leaders, around which to forge an *anti*-imperial identity; and in the case of the latter a feminine one, to boot. Lastly, there was the awkward fact of the Roman Empire's 'decline and fall', chronicled at great length by Edward Gibbon in the 1770s and '80s, the book itself written so stylishly and becoming so popular as to overshadow all accounts of the rise of the Roman Empire, and so drawing more attention to its failures than was perhaps fair.[2] In British history the period after the departure of the Romans, and before Britain's new set of brutal 'civilisers' landed in 1066, was dubbed the 'Dark Ages', which could point two contradictory lessons: either the necessity of empire to keep things going ('if only we'd stayed on in Zimbabwe', or wherever); or the flaws in imperialism as a permanent method of building 'civilisation'. For late-Victorian British imperialists unwilling to accept either of these lessons, it was cautionary, at least. By avoiding the mistakes of the Romans, maybe the British Empire's decline and fall could be forestalled. It may be significant that Thomas Thornycroft's heroic equestrian statue near Westminster Bridge of 'Boadicea' and her daughters (beaten and raped by the Romans), and Edward Elgar's *Caractacus* oratorio both appeared in public at a time – around 1900 – when doubts about the longevity and indeed survival of the British Empire were starting to hove into view.

British imperialism was usually distinguished from all previous sorts, therefore, by being presented as uniquely 'liberal', or 'humanitarian'; its ultimate purpose being to teach its subject peoples to fly the nest and look after themselves. This obviously avoided any danger of the 'fall' scenario; for by this way of looking at it the 'fall' of the British Empire would – like the destruction of the cocoon around a caterpillar – also be its greatest success. Lord Macaulay once wrote that nothing would give him, or the British, greater pride than the moment when the Indian butterfly became free.[3] It would mark not the failure of imperialism, but its culmination. Of course, it would take time – several generations at least – for all those millions of 'natives' to become (as Macaulay saw it) sufficiently anglicised, meaning that perhaps current colonial rulers need not bother their heads too much about it from day to day, which of course raises doubts about their sincerity. But in most imperialist credos of this time the idea of a liberationist empire, linking together what were generally regarded as the antitheses of *Imperium et Libertas* (one imperialist wrote a book with this title[4]), was the crucially distinctive feature of it. The Romans worked with native collaborators (Cunobelinus in Britain, for example: Shakespeare's *Cymbeline*); but not with any deliberate intention of handing rule over to them ultimately. That was what gave the British hope that their empire might last for longer than the Roman, possibly even for ever in one form or another – in George Bernard Shaw's *Back to Methuselah* (1921) it's still there in the year 3000, but ruled now from Baghdad – or at least that its winding up would not be regarded as a defeat or a disgrace.

That was necessary in order to reconcile what in certain academic circles is called the 'imperial discourse' of the time with another, the 'liberal' one, which was arguably far more dominant in Britain, at least at social levels beneath the upper classes. 'Freedom' was absolutely central to most British people's sense of national identity from at least the eighteenth century on, defined in various different and even contradictory ways (one man's economic freedom is another's capitalist tyranny, for example), but built around the idea of the 'free Briton', subject to equal laws, king in his own castle, with some part (albeit indirect) in his own government, and 'never never never' being a slave. ('His', because women were usually excluded.) Britain's history was taught – to the middle classes at least – as a story of 'progress' in a liberal direction, from Magna Carta (or perhaps the Saxon Witangemot) onwards; occasionally uneven, with the Normans, Stuarts and Lord Liverpool's government in the 1810s and '20s setting it back temporarily, but always winning through at last. (This was Seeley's gripe: that there was no imperial history to balance this.) This was what marked Britain off from other European countries, with the result, for example, that she escaped most of the latter's great social conflagrations, especially 1848, and was able to stage a great international display like the Great Exhibition only three years later with only happy Britons looking on; and why in particular her Queen was so popular, symbolising as she did enlightened, constitutional and consequently 'free' government. (Over the course of her reign three or four potshots were taken at her; on each of those occasions the assailant was officially adjudged insane, as he had to be.) Much of this 'freedom' may have been quite illusory: again, it depends how you look at it. But it was essential to ordinary Britons' self-image, and for the purposes of their real rulers, who needed them to be happily compliant, to believe that this was what marked their country off from nearly all the rest.

If 'imperialism' *was* a national discourse – and in fact there were several – then it had to fit in with this much older and more resilient one. 'Liberal imperialism' was one way of doing this. Later, in the early twentieth century, it morphed into a new kind of 'imperialism', called the 'Commonwealth idea', by Britain's pretending that her empire was essentially a voluntary association, not an essentially 'imperial' one at all. ('Please may we join your empire?') That could be seen as a case of the liberal discourse trumping the imperial one, and may indicate its potency all along. In the end it was the contradiction between the two discourses that contributed to the Empire's problems in the middle of the twentieth century, and it was one of the reasons – as we shall see later – why the British Empire came to an end.

It is worth pausing here to remember that 'imperialism' had two meanings in the later nineteenth century: one expansionary, the other to do with ruling the empire you had. Most liberal imperialists were of the latter sort, wishing to improve the existing British Empire, rather than seize more colonies. But there *were* ways in which liberalism can be seen to have helped drive the more aggressive imperial project on. It depended on how universal you believed the particular form of liberalism you had discovered was. If the only proper form of liberalism was the one that embraced free elections, free trade, freedom of thought and the rest on the British pattern, or one very close to it, then it would seem churlish and time-wasting merely to leave other countries free to find these truths off their own bats, when, by taking them over, you could present them to them fully formed. Many liberals were of this mind; in common, of course, with other ideologues: French revolutionism and Soviet Bolshevism are two other 'universal' belief systems that took imperialistic forms. It is for this reason, basically, that even expansionary imperialism was (and is) at least as compatible (in the British context) with a left-wing as a right-wing politics, with 'conservatives' generally being less culturally arrogant, more tolerant of alternative ways, customs and forms of rule; as well as – if they remain true to the literal meaning of *that* 'c'-word – less keen on 'change'. (Not all Conservatives have been conservative, of course, especially in recent years.) Joseph Chamberlain, a radical Liberal who turned radical imperialist in the 1880s, was not such an oddity as he was widely taken to be at the time, especially by his former Liberal colleagues, who regarded his switch of parties – to an alliance with the Conservatives – as 'treachery'. It wasn't necessarily, in ideological terms.

It did, however, tuck him up with some strange bedfellows: radical Conservatives whose imperialism was not 'liberal' at all, but had entirely different roots. Some of these can be seen as throwbacks to a previous, pre-liberal age, as that Austrian sociologist (Joseph Schumpeter) regarded all modern imperialists; fired by old ideas of military glory, hierarchy and national prestige. This shows how lively that other – pre-capitalist – head of our monster could be, despite its marginality to the major, liberal trend of the times. Sometimes it was so marginal as to be actually foreign. One of the most prolific British imperial propagandists of the turn of the twentieth century was a German, J. O. Eltzbacher, who changed his name to 'J. Ellis Barker' to disguise the fact.[5] Another was a great French admirer of the British Empire, and also, incidentally, of the English public schools.[6] The major organiser of 'imperial exhibitions' in Britain around then was a Hungarian, Imre Kiralfy; as were, a little later, the Korda brothers, who made most of those swashbuckling interwar imperial films. Others were either Anglo-Irish: Lord Meath, for example, who started the 'Empire Day' movement; or Anglo-Indian, like Rudyard Kipling, the great imperial *skald*. In these cases the hyphens denoted a certain distance from the British cultural mainstream, which almost certainly had something to do with their unconventional outlooks. Alfred (later Lord) Milner, one of the most 'Prussian' of British imperialists – as contemporaries remarked – had been educated in Germany. The most 'British' of these conservative empire cheerleaders came from the upper and military classes, as readers of this book up till now will have come to expect; and which also set them apart from ordinary folk.

Conservative imperialists mainly regarded the British Empire as a sign and source of power and glory: they loved the ceremony and flummery of it all; or else – and this became a growing theme during the closing years of the nineteenth century – they considered it essential for defending and securing Britain herself against foreign threats. Around this time Conservatives became much troubled, even obsessed, by certain great geopolitical tendencies they began to discern whereby, in a nutshell, the future of the world lay with powers possessing great territories and resources, which Britain, of course, did not have *without* her empire, which was the only thing enabling her to compete. Some right-wing future scenarios (in one of the golden ages, incidentally, of novelistic science fiction and futurology) were downright alarming: Gustave Doré's famous engraving of a future New Zealander gazing on the ruins of London, for example; and various predictions of Britain being invaded or even merely outperformed by an expansionist Germany; followed by Russia, America and Japan; with after that Islam ('Mohammedan fanaticism') and China (pretty accurate, so far); and culminating in H. G. Wells's Martians landing on Horsell Common, north of Woking (1897).[7] The last, of course, was not taken seriously, at least until it was dramatised on American radio by Orson Welles in 1938 (perhaps the most notorious invasion panic of all); but the others struck chords, and the general thesis behind them – that 'big' equalled 'strong and safe' – seemed convincing. People were still grappling with Darwin's 'struggle of the fittest' idea, after all, recently adapted to human societies by the philosopher Herbert Spencer, and given a geopolitical twist by the geographer (and imperialist) Halford Mackinder: 'he who controls the heartland' – central Asia – 'controls the world'. As things were, Britain had an interest there; but not if she lost India and her influence in the Middle East. In 1908 the ex-Viceroy of India Lord Curzon predicted that without her empire Britain would decline to the status of a 'merely' European country, like 'little Belgium'.[8] God forbid.

This right-wing brand of imperialism didn't stop there. It also took on social and political dimensions. Maintaining the Empire in these ominous modern circumstances, let alone extending it, would involve all the efforts of Britain's relatively small population, which would need to be harnessed, therefore, specifically to that end. This might be difficult at a time when, according to dozens of alarmist reports, the British people as a whole were 'deteriorating', as it was put, both physically and mentally. The generally poor health of young men and boys from the inner cities was highlighted, and in an imperial context, by an inquiry into why so many volunteers – *volunteers*, mark – for the army, to fight the war in South Africa, had had to be rejected on physical grounds, which was reported in 1904 with some worrying statistics. At the same time there were reports of increasing insanity, suicide, homosexuality (the 'Oscar Wilde tendency') and self-abuse (how could they tell?); mounting Jewish immigration; as well as rumours of workshyness and lack of patriotism, fears of the effects of football as a spectator sport on young males, young women 'shirking their duties' (to breed new little male soldiers); and of course socialism, which involved putting class loyalty before imperial.[9] This last was also thought to be reflected in the politics of the day, where narrow *party* loyalties trumped patriotism. All this added up to a serious problem at the 'Heart of the Empire' (the title of another contemporary imperialist tract),[10] which would need deep surgery to put it right.

Hence, right-wing imperialism in Britain became associated, from the 1890s onwards, with a whole range of policies, not all of which seemed to have a direct relation to the Empire itself. 'Tariff reform' – the return of duties on imports into Britain – did, because it was tied in with a pet scheme of Chamberlain's to unite the whole Empire in a great free-trade zone (or '*Zollverein*', after the German customs union that had helped unite that country), in order to protect the British economy against competition from the new and larger powers. So did the movement, led by Field Marshal Lord Roberts, to introduce military conscription in Britain for the first time in a hundred years. The idea of setting up rifle clubs to train a military citizenship in national defence – and at the same time tempt it away from the football terraces – pointed in the same direction. And Meath's idea of a national 'Empire Day' to celebrate the British Empire once a year in schools was manifestly relevant. Sometimes this relevance could have been misleading. All these vaguely militaristic ideas also had other obvious advantages: especially to industrialists, if it helped to discipline their workforces too. It may be significant that the original version of Baden-Powell's Boy Scout promise was to 'do their duty' not only to 'God and the King', but to their 'employers' too.[11] That was ditched later; but it may indicate another motive for many of these schemes, lurking beneath the overtly 'imperial' one.

Others were less openly imperialist. 'Social reform', for example, could only be regarded as such at one remove; which was why many Labour MPs allied themselves with 'social imperialists' on this. 'I know it sounds terribly like rank Socialism', wrote one of the latter; but 'I know it to be first-class Imperialism too.'[12] Not all right-wing imperialists swallowed this. Some thought the solution to the 'social problem' that was endangering the Empire, by which they mainly meant the problem of the stunted and feckless working classes, was to impose more discipline on them; or, *in extremis*, simply to weed them out. That was the 'eugenic' solution; fashionable in some circles at this time, though it never caught on practically as it did in Nazi Germany, Sweden and some southern US states. The furthest that most British imperialists would go was to deny the wastrels welfare. 'No other nation,' claimed Lord Meath, 'maintains an army of paupers out of the enforced taxation of the industrious.'[13] There were obvious class advantages to that too. But it was hardly likely to catch on as an electoral slogan: 'let the runts die'. It may have been too early for that.

This, however, simply highlighted another problem – elections. Many right-wing imperialists were fundamentally anti-democratic, whether overtly or – surely – in their guts. This was not an unusual position at this time (the later nine-teenth century), when democracy for men had only been half-achieved, and for women not at all. It is interesting how many of the leading opponents of women's suffrage in the early 1900s were prominent imperialists, including several women. For them a particular problem operated here: what female legislator would vote for an imperial war, however necessary, if it put their dear little sons in the line of fire? (That question was pretty conclusively answered in 1982.) But the imperial loyalties of working-class men were also generally distrusted, though some professed to believe that at bottom the stout-hearted prole was as patriotic as anyone, if you could only drag his ear away from those seductive socialists. (The same was often said of colonial subjects: loyal to a man and a woman, but led astray by nationalist agitators.) Democracy was thought to be inimical to imperialism, whether it really was or not. Quite apart from that, the structure of the political process in Britain did not conduce to patriotic decisions, deliberately confrontational as it was, with two sets of benches facing one another, and organised into 'parties'; fatal, it was thought, to consensual policies on anything. Several imperialists advocated abolishing the House of Commons altogether, in favour of an Empire-wide federal Parliament of trusted imperial statesmen, or a new House of Lords leavened with some of the last. Short of that, perhaps Liberal and Conservative imperialist MPs could team up to run the country patriotically from the middle. (Except that it wasn't really the 'middle'.) At any rate, something needed to be done. Later on it may have been done in a different way entirely; with government becoming distanced and hidden from the 'democracy', in ways that will be suggested later.

In the end, in fact, *none* of these things was done before the Great War, with the exception of those social reforms that the social*ists* accepted too. That of course made right-wing imperialists even more depressed, and even desperate, with a group of them actually backing an army mutiny in Ireland in March 1914 in protest against the imminent granting of 'Home Rule' there: the thin end of a wedge, as they saw it. One of the great 'what might have beens' of British history has always been how the socialist and trade union movements – pretty militant in the years leading up to 1914 – might have developed if there had been no war; but the same could be asked of the powerful, reactionary, right-wing movements of the time too. However, the War changed all that. Both of the forms of ideological imperialism outlined here survived it, as did, of course, the Empire – albeit with difficulty, as we shall see. But they emerged in different strengths, with the liberal one dominating, in the form of 'Commonwealthism'; and the Conservative one coming, eventually, to be perceived as a bit of a joke – though not to the people whom it affected still.

The main way that imperialists of both general persuasions tried to push their agendas was through propaganda, of which there was a great deal in Britain from the 1880s on. It was manifested in a score of forms: most prominently literature, the music hall, films and exhibitions, but also, maybe more subliminally, in areas like advertising, of almost anything, and consumer items that were Empire-sourced. The classic work on this is John MacKenzie's

Propaganda and Empire (1984), and the nearly hundred volumes that it spawned in MacKenzie's own (edited) 'Studies in Imperialism' series. Much of it was directed at juveniles, mostly boys but also some for girls (who would be expected to dutifully assist their brothers and future husbands in upholding the Empire, in ways appropriate to their sex), with some popular novelists pumping out several dozens of colonial-set 'ripping yarns' for adolescents in the course of their careers. For younger children there were imperial wooden toys, and 'ABCs' of Empire. ('V: Here is Queen Victoria, In all her regalia, One foot in Canada, The other in Australia.'[4]) There were also imperial magazines and Christmas annuals. And around 1900, for almost the first time, the Empire was taken on board by some schools in their history classes: often pushing the genesis of the 'Empire' back to Elizabethan times to give it a more solid genealogy. Adults are supposed to have been stimulated – even to the extent of 'jingoism' – by patriotic music-hall songs. Imre Kiralfy's pre-1914 Empire exhibitions, and then the big official one of 1924 at Wembley (a road near Wembley Stadium is still called 'Empire Way'), served all age groups. There were 'newsreel' films of British imperial wars in the 1890s (usually faked on an English common somewhere), and later a fair number of feature films on imperial themes. (Perhaps the most resonantly imperialist of them, though it is fairly late – it was made in 1959 – is *North West Frontier*, starring Kenneth More.) Popular newspapers like the *Daily Mail* and the *Daily Express* churned out their proprietors' imperialistic views, as one has grown to expect in recent years. In the case of the *Express* the owner was a Canadian. Even serious classical composers couldn't entirely resist some imperial 'pomp and circumstance', though Elgar's overtly imperial pieces are uncharacteristic, and don't seem to have his heart in them. If you couldn't imperialise the nation through legislation, this was how you had to do it: culturally, from beneath. A great deal of this went on in the 1900s, and hardly stopped until the 1960s. How effective it was is controversial, and will be discussed in a later chapter.

When it did have an effect it was in a particular way. By the interwar period the Empire was presented not primarily as a site of conquest, far less of exploitation, but as something far more benevolent. By then the 'liberationist' narrative had all but triumphed, and people back home were taught that the whole point of the Empire was to 'develop' its peoples; with a commercial pay-off to Britain too, of course, but there was not necessarily any contradiction there. Beyond that there were so many other benefits that Britain could bring them: teaching them how different races and religions could live together, for example; why should Hindus and Muslims, or Jews and Arabs, or black and white in East Africa, be less capable of this than the English and Scots – still of course happily united then? Ultimately the prospect held out to them, when they had all 'developed' sufficiently, was of living as a confederation of equal nations, with Britain simply as *primus inter pares*, or a kind of 'mother' figure; bound in friendship in this new multiracial 'Commonwealth', which the British saw as a kind of happier United Nations in miniature.

A lot of that was self-deception, or wishful thinking. But not everyone was deceived. Around the turn of the century a number of events in one or other of the colonies themselves served to prick the illusion: like the South African War, of course, but also 'atrocities' revealed in Egypt and the German colonies, and the greatest atrocity of them all – 'King Leopold's Congo', that inferno of European exploitation and cruelty. It is worth noting that the great public protest movement against that (the Congo Reform Association) originated and was orchestrated in Britain.[15] This must serve to modify, to an extent at any rate, the image of Britain as an essentially and predominantly 'imperialist' country. Of course she was: indeed, the leading imperial nation of that time; but that didn't prevent – it may even have helped – her also becoming the leading and indeed original *anti*-imperialist one. She is not always given the credit for that – if 'credit' is the right word.

A word of explanation may be necessary here. 'Anti-imperialism' is being used here in a very precise sense. Of course, peoples have been protesting and struggling against their *own* domination or threatened domination by imperial powers from time immemorial. The English are an example, in Roman and then in Viking and Norman times. The Welsh and Scots too. Britain has a long tradition of this. World War II was the last example. Anti-globalisation and Europhobia might be two others. Going even further back, I'm sure the Neanderthals put up a bit of a struggle before they were replaced by the new African-origin Cro-Magnons, in – when was it? – around 20,000 BCE. Modern-day Americans claim that they are a fundamentally anti-imperialist nation because they rebelled against their British imperial yoke; but that, of course, was only in order to be able to create an empire of their own. (They were quite open about this, from the start.) We have seen that at that time, and up to then, empires were regarded as 'natural'. They were almost never criticised or opposed *qua* empires, but only for the ways they used or abused their imperial powers, in each victim's particular case. It is in this sense that we can say that anti-imperialism *in principle* only begins around the turn of the twentieth century; and in Britain – the most extensive imperial power at that time – especially. It was able to draw on a long and rich radical and democratic heritage, which had always been at loggerheads with more authoritarian and imperialist discourses. That's when the tail started to wag; weakly at first, but then more vigorously, shaking the body away.

Before that, however, it is important to be aware of the idealistic aspects of the British Empire, which were not all illusory. If it was a monster, it still had some cuddly bits. The 'Commonwealth' ideal was not a sordid one. It could be argued – counter-intuitively, perhaps, but it *was* argued by the great predatory imperialist Cecil Rhodes – that imperialism conduced to peace. (Rhodes's argument was that wars were fought between nations. If every country subsumed its nationality into the British Empire – first on Rhodes's list was the United States, which he hoped could be lured back – there would be no more wars. Naive, perhaps, and of course we can't trust Rhodes himself to

have been sincere about this; but not ignoble in principle.[16])
Many imperialists who put their careers where their mouths
were, and actually went out to 'serve' their colonial subjects
'in the field', were inspired more by such ideals than by the
hope of material gain, which as civil servants they were not
allowed in any case. All they could expect from half a life-
time spent in colonial service, usually in trying conditions
and circumstances, was a comfortable salary, long holidays,
some prestige, the gratitude of their wards, and the knowledge thereafter, as they sipped their gin and tonics back in
the Home Counties, of a job – in their eyes – well done.
Whatever the impact on the world of the British Empire's
great idealistic projects may have been – let us leave that
question open for the moment – still these men (and their
subordinate women) did very many small good things. We
shall turn to those next.

FOUR

In the Field

O F COURSE, 'imperialism' worked out differently on the ground. One obvious reason was the obstacles and distractions it had to deal with there. Another was that in this area of government, as in many others, practice only had a very tenuous connection with 'policy', and even more so with the 'ideas' behind that. A third was that the people who were supposed to put those ideas and policies into practice were a rum lot, a species (and several sub-species) of their own. One must not make the mistake of assuming that Britain's representatives in the colonial field accurately mirrored the society from which they came. Even if some of them reflected certain aspects and classes of it when they went out there, many were changed radically by their experiences in the colonies. This was why, when they took furloughs or retirement in Britain, they found it difficult to fit back in. Some, in fact, didn't try, but retired among their former subjects, whom they felt they got on with better.

In any case, they represented no typical class or group of people back in Britain, apart from those like them.

For a start, they were nearly all men. Women weren't allowed into the Colonial or Indian Civil Services until very late on; unsurprisingly in that age of acknowledged and of course deliberate gender discrimination. They could, however, have imperial roles as missionaries, medical workers and, of course, wives. In the case of the men, secondly, they may have been distinctive sexually, with many gay men among them, though it is impossible, of course, to estimate how many. It is the historian Ronald Hyam's thesis that the colonies represented a refuge for men (and a few women) with unconventional, excessive or illegal sexual preferences, attracted there by the relative sexual licence tolerated by other, less morally uptight cultures than Britain's; and of course by the power they had to exploit them.[1] (A student once suggested to me that this could be called the 'swollen gonads' theory of imperialism.) Thirdly, colonial workers were unbalanced nationally, with Scots being rather over-represented, especially in India. (In fact the British Empire was far more a Scottish than an English one, from many points of view. Don't believe present-day Scots who present themselves as colonial victims; which may be considered more respectable nowadays, but is untrue in their case.[2]) On the other hand they didn't include many outright foreigners, unlike the Congo 'Free' State with all its free-floating Swedes.

So far as both English and Scottish colonialists were concerned, a significant number of them appear to have come from the interstices between the classes of society, rather than the solid middles of the middle or upper ranks; people who were insecure in their class situation in Britain, from which the colonies offered an escape. Missionaries are a clear example, many of them coming from the *aspirant* (usually nonconformist) working classes; but it is surprising how many other imperial actors, when you look into their backgrounds, were also unsettled and uncomfortable class-wise. The explorers Livingstone and Stanley are leading examples, Stanley in spades: illegitimate, Welsh, part American; as well as empire builders like Raffles (of Singapore), who had to work his way up and was snubbed terribly by 'real' gentlemen when he was made a knight. The same, incidentally, can be said of the class origins of Britain's leading artists, like Turner, Elgar and Dickens; although in as philistine a country as Britain was in their time, it would have been difficult for any artist to fit in. Is this a general rule? Or is it, perhaps, that more Britons were dissatisfied with their social situations than appearances would suggest? One day, perhaps, a PhD student with a competence in British social as well as imperial history, and a head for statistics, might like to take this up. And if there is something in it, what might be the reason? Was it this that gave these interstitials the urge to be different? In any case, they *were* different, and (I would say) more interesting than the comfortable bankers or shopkeepers they left behind, or the proles who 'knew their place'. Whatever the answers, this must serve at least to throw doubt on any idea that Britain abroad was just an extension of Britain at home; or, if it was at the beginning of a chap's service in the colonies, that it remained like that for long.

Again, it depended who, where and when they were. The most recognisable of them, of course, were colonial officers: the men who were sent out to the colonies to rule. With regard to them, however, we first need to get out of the way the 'settlement' colonies, where British colonial rule was minimal. White men were supposed to be able to rule themselves (and their women). They were also, as we have seen, entrusted with the governance of native minorities, though with a patina, at any rate, of supervision from Whitehall, through 'native commissioners' and the like. These were usually well disposed towards the natives, as were many of the colonial governors; but were generally ineffective in reining back greedy or fearful settlers. It was largely a question of means: colonial administrations were very thinly manned, and lightly armed. Otherwise, most 'white' colonies had governors, with small secretarial staffs, but governing through locally elected parliaments. In fact, colonial settlers enjoyed more effective democracy than most of the folk they had left behind in Britain. (So they should have had no complaints.) That was why they were admired and envied by British radicals, and greatly distrusted by the upper classes, whose kind of empire this wasn't at all. Governors were chosen from a variety of different groups, including Colonial Office personnel in London; military and naval men; lower-rank diplomats – lower because the colonies had very little kudos; and local people. This general system covered all the European-majority colonies, including British

North America (Canada), the Australian colonies, and New Zealand.

It was also however extended to cover several colonies where there weren't really enough settlers to take the burden of government off the Colonial Office's hands, or at least to exercise it, with regard to the natives, in a way that would satisfy humanitarian opinion back home. In one notable case of a local black rebellion this led the Colonial Office to take a colony – Jamaica – away from the settlers (in this case planters and ex-slave-owners) who had run it previously, and return it to direct British rule. That probably should also have been done in the case of (Southern) Rhodesia in the 1960s, but was thought to be too difficult at the time. Even the titular governor there had no authority at all. In neighbouring South Africa it was partially done by reserving the administration of certain parts of it, called the 'High Commission Territories', to the Crown, but only after the rest of the country had been given over to the white minority, and on racist terms (1906–10). It is no coincidence that these were, as we shall see later, the sites of some of the most bloody rebellions and repression during the time of 'decolonisation'. ('Privatisation', again.) Other colonies ruled with only a light touch were the 'Princely States' of India; some 'Protectorates', where the idea was not that Britain should rule there but simply that no *other* imperial nation should; colonies that were simply neglected; and a number – notably Northern Nigeria – ruled 'indirectly' in principle; that is because it was thought better, for philosophical as well as practical reasons, to let people rule themselves along their own lines. We shall return to this shortly.

That left the mainly tropical colonies (including huge Nigeria) and India to be governed directly, by a *profession* of imperial rulers. Or rather two, because India and the rest of the Empire had their own governing cultures, and almost no personnel in common. (People didn't generally switch from one service to the other.) India was easily the most prestigious of the two, although in the twentieth century the Sudan, which had a separate civil service of its own (British imperial rule really was very muddled), rivalled it in reputed intellectual quality. India had the prestigious Haileybury in Hertfordshire (and the lesser 'Westward Ho!' in Devon: Kipling's alma mater) to train her potential rulers up, including in Indian history and languages; and a stiff exam for them to pass. From 1858 Indians were technically able to compete for this, though practical obstacles made that exceedingly rare. The Colonial Service was strikingly differ-ent, with a much more informal entry system, even when a keen new 'Recruiting Officer', Sir Ralph Furse (Eton and Balliol, Oxford), was appointed to vet applicants properly in 1919. (He stayed until 1948.) Furse wasn't at all impressed by 'cleverness' – the story went that he deliberately turned down one candidate who had left a copy of *The Times* with the crossword filled in prominently on his chair in the waiting room – preferring what he, and so many others of the public-school set at that time, called 'character'.[3] The initial handshake was crucial; a 'limp wrist' would damn anyone. As a fourth-class brain himself (only Oxford gave fourth-class degrees), he favoured more rounded, stable and loyal sorts of chaps, like himself. School (usually the 'lesser' public ones), games and family were also important indicators of worth. It was such people, by and large, who were sent out to govern the Crown colonies, each of them responsible for hundreds of thousands of subjects. One has to admire their nerve, if nothing else.

Actually there is a lot more to admire. Retired colonial civil servants in the 1960s and '70s (I talked to a number of them then) used to be quite pained when in the general 'anti-imperialist' atmosphere of the time they were put down as the villains of the piece. They were not that. There were some bad apples, as the cliché goes, who 'went bad in the tropics', as their contemporaries more often put it; with the occasional report of a District Officer's paedophile activities, for example,[4] but many more probably hidden away or destroyed afterwards, as we know many colonial papers were, to safeguard Britain's reputation: with the result that we cannot possibly tell how far this sort of thing went. They themselves put great weight on their 'honour', altruism and incorruptibility, however, which they believed distinguished them from other colonisers, and especially the Germans and Belgians, who stood as perpetual examples of a whole system going bad. They also prided themselves on their relations with 'their' natives, which had to be harmonious at one level because of their essential vulnerability, and limited means. (The Colonial Office didn't like to have to send troops in.) The harmony, however, was usually of a patronising kind, like that of a father towards his children, or a good master towards his servants, at best; which is how the colonial class generally looked on other peoples – its own working classes, incidentally, as well as those of other 'races'. Many of them developed a real affection for the people they were ruling, though rarely on equal terms, and possibly only because of the latter's deference. A few 'went native', though that was frowned upon. Nearly all of them found willing native collaborators to work with. Some learned native languages. Generally they just pottered on, travelling all over in their distinctive pith or safari helmets, sorting out disputes, dispensing justice, supervising building projects and collecting taxes when they dared to levy them. (There was little that was more likely to provoke rebellions.) Most of them assumed that they and their successors would still be doing these things far into the future, even when all the signs should have told them otherwise. When the penny finally dropped, they sincerely regretted that they hadn't been given more time to tidy things up before Britain 'scuttled'. Most of them blamed the 'bloody Yanks' for that.[5]

This highlighted one of their great deficiencies, which was a certain lack of imagination, possibly deriving from the fact that they *weren't* the brightest buttons in the imperial box. Their public-school educations emphasised the virtues of conformity and loyalty as essential elements towards the great pedagogical object of 'character formation'; together with overcoming hardships, team spirit, not 'sneaking', suppressing emotions, taking beatings without blubbing, and a bit of Greek. This may be why they couldn't see what they were doing in any kind of context, apart from the colonial one they had set out with. They weren't inquisitive, or very creative. Very few new ideas about colonial government came up from this level. Most of these came from the outside, or above.

That may be generalising far too blandly about a group of people who must have had some exceptions among them; but the comparative work just hasn't been done on them yet. Many of the same generalisations apply to the Indian Civil Service (ICS), whose staff had a stronger *esprit de corps* than their co-workers in the colonies, and were always more 'romantic' – not their own doing, but deriving mainly from the fabulous native cultural environment in which they found themselves – and so were, and have been subsequently, far more written about. One of the best accounts, by someone who lived there (as secretary to a maharajah), is E. M. Forster's *A Passage to India* (1924), which is very largely *about* the varieties of Briton to be found there. Like colonial rulers, but more so, they tended to come from closed lines or families, some of them going back to Company days, and consequently were a very distinctive set, cut off even more from their compatriots back home. 'Anglo-Indians' (the term had two meanings; this is the one referring to Britons living in India) were a separate subspecies of Brit from any of the mainland ones, much as the Anglo-Irish were. From their fathers and mothers, their special schools, but much more from the environments in which they were placed in India, they took on the qualities that distinguished them. Among these (again, to generalise shamelessly) were a degree of arrogance, necessary it was thought to maintain your dignity and authority; a damaging 'white man's club' culture in the major Indian conurbations; an authoritarian mindset; but also, quite often – it is illustrated in Forster's book – a growing empathy with these ancient and outwardly impressive civilisations they hardly felt mature enough in their own 'civilisation' to be lording it over. The last is evidenced by the numbers of them who, again, remained behind in India after decolonisation, and not only because they could carry on their own styles of life there (India was cheaper, and you could easily find servants), but also because of a genuine admiration and liking for Indians. Talk with many Indians after independence – I was at college with several of them – and they could express an unexpected affection for their former masters. (Of course, the ones I was at college with probably came from the 'collaborating' Indian classes before independence.) The ICS seems to have been fairly generously leavened with mavericks, who had managed to break out of the old-school *esprit de corps*.

Evident with all these men, because they were men, was what today we call a 'masculinist' discourse; and the same is true of their womenfolk – those attached to the sahibs, that is, as wives or daughters – who nearly always took on the attitudes of their husbands and fathers while they were with them. This was partly a racial thing; one of the excuses for Britain's lording it over the Indians was that they were the masculine *race*, with the Indians – many of them; usually not the Muslims – a feminine one, which meant that wives had to act in dominant, manly ways in front of the 'natives', if not in their own homes. 'Masculinism' included all those virtues taught in the boys' public schools – the 'character' thing; but there was also another element to it as well, which might be described as 'parentalism'. This is what is generally referred to as 'paternalism', but it was indistinguishable really from the roles that mothers usually play, in protecting and doing their best for their wards. The point to make is that it was a rather gentler and more nurturing role than that usually associated with the 'masculine' qualities; and that it was as much a part of these men's public-school education as the 'hardening' thing. It derived from the idea of 'service'; which in its turn had come down from the 'feudal' or 'aristocratic' roots of this part of the British 'hybrid'. It was the other face of the monster, trying to put on a smile.

The more individualistic and therefore interesting sorts of imperialists in the eighteenth, nineteenth and twentieth centuries – usually the 'interstitial' ones – were the traders, settlers, explorers, missionaries and other professionals who accompanied, or sometimes preceded, the rulers. (This of course is to use the word 'imperialist' in one of its looser ways.) What they were out there for is obvious in most cases; although when you start delving down into genuine 'motivations' the picture can get muddier. (It has occurred to many of us more coddled observers that, in the case of the great explorers, for example, masochism must have played a part.) What is important to note is that it was these *functions*, in general, that governed their attitudes towards the countries they were in and, especially, their peoples. Often the assumption is made that they went out from Britain as what is called 'racists', the racism having been inculcated in their homes and schools. That may not have been so; and to the extent that it was, it could be modified or changed. Colonial Britons' race attitudes depended far more on what they were supposed to be doing among the 'races' – their 'functions' – than on what their minds had been set up to think.

In the case of the rulers, for example, their whole rationale, to protect and hopefully 'improve' the natives, depended on the natives being worth protecting, and ultimately improvable. They also required them to help in all this. (Again, we should not forget how very few British rulers in the field there were.) District Officers in Africa therefore tended to appreciate the more loyal and grateful of them – the 'doggy' ones – for that reason, and quite irrespective of 'race'; back in Britain they regarded their own working classes in exactly the same way. Similarly, again, to the situation in Britain, they regarded nationalist 'agitators' – like socialist agitators – as *atypical* of the general population, and so to be opposed and even loathed; again, not on racial grounds necessarily. Race attitudes among these men scarcely differed from the class attitudes they had imbibed at home, and in their schools; stuck as they were – as the dullest and most conformist of the latter's graduates – with the attitudes that Furse had selected them for.

They could also be remarkably tolerant of and even impressed by native cultures, and especially hierarchies, partly as a result of the difficulties they met in trying to 'anglicise' them – shortage of staff, again – and the need therefore to find other ways to administer them. In the early 1900s this was a major factor behind the adoption in some colonies of a new method of government called 'indirect rule' – actually it wasn't all that new; Jesus had been crucified under a form of it, and there were plenty of British imperial precedents – which involved ruling not only through native hierarchies, but on native cultural lines. That of course went strongly against the 'anglicising' project, and annoyed other groups of (informal) imperialists, for whom changing the natives' cultures was the key to everything. The main objectors here were the missionaries, whose *cultural* prejudices were far stronger than their racial ones: 'racism' and what might be termed 'culturism' are often confused, and the one might sometimes be a cover for the other; but there is a theoretical difference between them at any rate. Missionaries were usually the least racist of any of these categories, *needing* to believe in the improvability of most other races in order to fulfil their function, and living up to their principles by elevating Africans to the very highest positions in their churches. (Bishop Samuel Ajayi Crowther of Nigeria was the most celebrated one.) Colonial officials didn't always go along with that. Christianity was not 'natural' to Africans, and could easily turn them into agitators. The East India Company banned missionaries from its possessions early on.

The settlers' and large-scale capitalists' functions turned them in a different direction entirely. To take the most extreme examples first: if you were a slave-owner or slave-driver, you again *needed* to believe the people you were enslaving were biologically inferior in order to justify forcing them to work for you. It was surely that way around; men didn't become slavers because they were racists, but vice versa. (In much the same way as a man doesn't become a banker because he's a Conservative, and I'm probably not an academic because I believe in free enquiry.) Much the same, although to a lesser degree, could be said of settlers who

needed rationales for seizing natives' lands and demand-
ing their labour; and industrialists who wanted excuses
for turning great areas of peasant-owned farming land
into plantations (as in the Congo). They, generally speaking, were the most disruptive and atrocity-prone of all the
colonial communities; and also the most race-prejudiced,
but mainly, again, due to their functions. Critics of the
latter – of the Congolese plantation 'concessionaires', for
example – claimed that this was not a necessary consequence
of capitalism. Pursued on a more modest level, through free
exchange with native middlemen, it could rub down racial
hostilities, with British traders and native customers sitting
down to enjoy a beer together at dusk after the haggling
was over. (Liverpool merchants were in the vanguard of
the movements against Leopold's Congo, and for 'peasant
proprietorship' *contra* plantations.) Again, it varied.

Other operators followed the same 'functional' rules.
Exploration could turn people's views of race two ways.
Isolated and highly vulnerable as they were in some of
the most unhealthy and dangerous places in the world,
travellers either had to live with their native neighbours,
or frighten them off, with guns. Both methods were used,
and attitudes swung accordingly between friendliness and
admiration (the usual one), and arrant racism. Soldiers are
some of the other villains in this picture, with their main
function being to kill people; often provoked by the people
who shot, or speared, them back; and of course with the
heat of battle to cope with. Military atrocities were (and
are still) as common as settler ones. Much of this was due
to the fact that soldiers rarely had much social contact with

the natives; except in India and one or two other places, where you had British officers commanding native troops. In these cases the bonds between the races in the same army could be close, if hardly equal. There are stories of Indian sepoys braving heavy fire to rescue their wounded officers, and vice versa; in exactly the same way as you would expect officers and men to behave towards each other in the British Army today.

Maybe the most enlightened imperial agents in this respect were the expert scientists sent out to advise colonial governments in the later nineteenth and twentieth centuries. Here you might have expected a very superior attitude from people in a field in which Western culture was undeniably ahead: you could differ over morals, religion and politics, but not surely over the superiority of Western science. Some cultural historians indeed maintain that is how it was: they came from racist Britain, after all; but when you look closely you find the scientists' attitudes changing, as they gained experience in the field. Agricultural and medical practices that were scorned came to be valued for their effectiveness, against all scientific expectations, and the scientists' textbooks rewritten as a result.[6] These are cases where any imperialist discourse they might have ingested in Britain became modified by experience in the colonies, and by their more powerful professional 'discourse', of empiricism, observation, experimentation and open-mindedness; so knocking on the head the notion that racial arrogance, in particular, was generated in Britain and then simply spread out.

Among the scientists was one group whose relationship with imperialism was ambivalent. Ethnologists (from *ethnos*: race or nation) worked on the assumption that there were ineradicable differences between 'races', which didn't necessarily signify a hierarchy of them, but was bound to imply it if your race was likely to take the top place if there was. They were often associated with skull-measuring. Late in the nineteenth century they became either renamed or displaced by 'anthropologists' (from *anthropos*: human), who studied human societies rather than racial characteristics, although – as in the case of our 'culturists' – the two might be elided by those who didn't know better. The anthropologists usually studied entire alien cultures from within; living amongst them and seeking to understand the underlying rationales, or 'latent' functions of customs that to Western minds often seemed irrational on the surface. The result of this was undoubtedly a greater sympathy with alien ways, which fitted in nicely with the 'indirect rule' scenario; but too well both for some colonial rulers, and for many colonial subjects. The rulers were sceptical because it seemed to rule out *all* reform. (Later British anthropology was tweaked a little, to include the 'anthropology of culture-change': that is, of the effects of cross-cultural contacts, where they seemed inevitable.[7]) Colonial nationalists objected because it seemed to be designed to cut them off from the Western progress that they now wanted, after having been taught its superiority for so long. 'Indirect rule' was suspected of being designed to keep them 'down'; as it was, in a way. (Later, South African apartheid, expressing much the same philosophy, could exemplify that.) Besides, being studied by 'anthropologists' appeared demeaning in itself. Obviously, it was only because they were 'primitive'. Why did anthropologists never look at Western societies? In 1934 one early black African administrator suggested this: that an African PhD candidate 'study the white peoples, especially the English, their customs and institutions, and interpret them to the world'.[8] *Touché*. It might be answered that Western scholars did study their own cultures, but called it 'sociology'. But in that case why was there any need for the separate nomenclature?

This was the problem, and one of the basic difficulties even with the best-intentioned 'imperialism'. Peoples don't always appreciate things being done *for* them. Even though anthropology as it developed in the early twentieth century was far more sensitive and sympathetic to other cultures than the common view of a homogeneously racist imperial discourse would suggest – *anti*-imperial in one sense, therefore – the Africans, or Indians, or whoever, didn't *own* it. It was for the same reason that some of the British Empire's successor states in the 1960s and '70s dumped many agricultural policies that had been developed by British agronomists, true, but on the basis of local traditional wisdoms, and for worthy ecological reasons. No matter; they weren't theirs. (Another reason may have been demands and bribes from capitalist 'developers'.) So it was difficult to know what to do right.

The broader lesson from all this is that British 'imperialism', in the widely assumed sense of the imposition of the imperial power's views and methods on its subjects, backed by an 'imperialist' sense of racial superiority in everything, was emphatically not the way it went everywhere. Sometimes that was tried; most notoriously and disastrously in India in the 1830s and '40s, when Britain – or rather, some of her provincial governors – suddenly developed, as a by-product of her 'Evangelical revival', an urge to 'Westernise' India thoroughly: her education, land ownership, religion, and so on. That provoked several revolts, culminating in the 'Great Mutiny' of 1857: called a 'mutiny' and not a rebellion, which is what it was, in order to diminish it; which was put down with blood and cruelty on both sides, and could have flung the British out. It was this that persuaded the British Parliament to take India under direct rule from the Company in 1858, and to tread more carefully from then on when it came to imposing its ways. Thereafter the British concentrated on material improvements – railways, harbours, dams, canals, and so on – which were what they were comfortable with: you didn't need to have much sensitivity for these; and simply keeping order; albeit with some resentment against the Indians' ingratitude, which lingered. 'Take up the White Man's burden, And reap his old reward; The blame of those ye better, The hate of those ye guard.' That was Kipling.[9] He knew; he came from there: another of those marginal men, in relation to mainland Britain, who turned out to be the most 'imperialist' of the British. It has a certain Roman dignity about it, which fitted in with the general right-wing pessimism of the time, and possibly the ethos – cold baths, beatings and all that – of the public schools. How much more brave and tough and honourable it was, after all, to struggle in a hopeless cause, without any thanks from those you were 'bettering', than merely to do the possible! It has a tragic but heroic ring to it. It was another, darker side to the 'feudal' head of our imperial monster; the idea of 'service' at its most extreme. But it did not come out of Britain, or *her* domestic culture; whose common takes on imperialism were very different, as a later chapter will hopefully show.

FIVE

How It Happened.
Broadly.

T HE EMPIRE served by these imperialists, both metropolitan and theoretical, and local and practical, was
not really of their making. Most ideological imperialists
came onto the scene only towards its end, after the Empire
had crept up on them unawares. Until then there was no
great imperial 'project' that statesmen followed and pushed
through. Most of Britain's accumulated possessions had
come to her in a variety of different ways: through trade
and emigration, as the spoils of war, as an unexpected side
effect of other actions and events, through preventing other
countries from monopolising them, or by 'invitation'; and,
if you consider it from the standpoint of the British state,
'accidentally'. Of course, 'accidental' is misleading; if British
governments rarely hankered for foreign possessions, they
usually wanted what those possessions brought with them,
and rarely (though they did sometimes) turned them down

when they came along. But 'imperialism', before the 1880s say, was never a deliberate policy. Nor was the expansion of the Empire, however it happened, necessarily a sign or source of Britain's growing strength in the world. Even with all her vast dominions, she never became a 'superpower'.

She certainly couldn't be described as that in the seventeenth and eighteenth centuries. She was becoming a great commercial nation. She was not alone in that. Peoples have always traded among themselves. England, Scotland and then (from 1707) Britain were no exceptions. Because of their island and oceanic situation much of this trade was done overseas, and from the late sixteenth century onwards very largely in new, 'undiscovered' regions of the world. ('Undiscovered', that is, by Europeans. The Native Americans, central Africans and Australian aboriginals knew where they were; though not necessarily in relation to the rest of the world.) They did this in common with several other European nations, and in fact about a century behind a couple of them. Asian countries were doing the same thing in their parts of the world. It was a 'global' phenomenon. Sometimes it involved taking over 'weaker' countries, out of avarice, because they wouldn't play ball otherwise, and/or because it was relatively easy. Rome had required great armies of centurions to extend its empire, but modern Europe didn't. Navies usually sufficed. By the eighteenth century five or six European nations had widespread possessions in the Americas, Asia and on the coasts of Africa; illustrated in microcosm by the Caribbean islands (named after the now disappeared Caribs), which boasted a variety of European national colours; or would have done, if anyone had thought of colour-coding imperial possessions then. Even Sweden had Saint-Barthélemy for a short while: sold to her by France in 1784, then given back in 1878. Such changes of sovereignty were quite common, especially after intra-European naval wars. The 'West Indies' were nearly all exploited with slave labour, captured in Africa (often by Arabs) and transported over, in notoriously horrendous conditions, in British and other ships. No one maritime European country, including Britain, was noticeably 'ahead' of any other colonially. In eastern North America Britain led France and Spain, the other main claimants, together of course with the dispossessed natives; but most of that 'empire' came to an end in 1783. Her other claim to imperial predominance was the East India Company's creeping control of the Indian subcontinent, which was challenged, however, by both France and the local Nawabs. Even that didn't begin to compete with the great Ottoman Empire, beginning its decline then, but still the largest and most feared at that time. (It used to enslave Europeans, for example.) This was broadly the situation until the end of the eighteenth century, when firstly the Industrial Revolution, and secondly Britain's first 'Great War', with France, kicked in.

The French wars had not been fought over 'empire', but they had the effect of removing France as a contender for India, and transferring a number of her little colonies to Britain. Thereafter all the seagoing European nations resumed their traffics with faraway places, including France, which in many cases led to a process that can be called 'creeping colonialism', in which little local crises provoked first of all local Europeans to intervene more proprietorially, and then their national armies to come in, more often than not reluctantly, to help them out. (Proud and militaristic France was probably the least reluctant.) Often these interventions were accompanied by savage reprisals, of the kind that has stained the reputation of 'imperialism' ever since. Naturally it was all rather downplayed at the height of imperialism, when its more benevolent side needed to be emphasised, but recently a number of blood-drenched books have come out to put the record straight.[1] These events embarrassed contemporary Britons, too, when they were known about: news took a very long time to get back from the East, remember; but apart from that Britain (meaning her government) was relatively unmoved by all this foreign colonial activity. Colonialism did not need to be competitive. There was plenty of room in the world for all. Foreign 'rivals' could be seen – as the old-fashioned Liberal Gladstone put it much later – as 'partners' with Britain in the extension of civilisation in the world to everyone's benefit.[2] So long as they didn't directly threaten Britain's interests she should be happy for them to take on the responsibility, and the expense.

The change came around the middle of the nineteenth century, after which it all became far less easy. The 1850s and '60s marked the peak of Britain's prosperity, relative to the rest of the world, often called, as they are, her 'Golden Years'. The sobriquet refers to her enormous industrial and commercial growth in this period, which appeared to be proving all those ideological free marketists – the Anti-Corn Law movement of the 1840s – right. It was ushered in by the hugely nationally self-confident Great Exhibition of 1851, which was meant to cock a friendly snook at Britain's competitors, by showing off all her great manufacturing achievements. (All the foreigners could put up against these were pretty arty things.) It was also a period of great optimism, wherever you stood in society, promising progress and growing prosperity all round. Even Marxists – both of them (him and Engels), who happened to be living in Britain at the time – believed things could go their way; *The Communist Manifesto*, published in English in 1850, is a highly optimistic work. The capitalist middle classes, of course, relied more on 'trickle down'. The number of 'improvements' taking place in this period – great building works, including (though unseen) London's marvellous and death-preventing sewage system, the first underground railway, the huge extension of overground railways, great steamships, medical breakthroughs, Pre-Raphaelitism and the Gothic Revival (if you consider these to be 'improvements'), the creation of the modern Liberal and Conservative parties, and a number of political reforms, usually 'liberating' one set of people or another, as well as much else – stood as testimony to this. The chauvinistic Palmerston was in his cocky prime. The Queen seemed happy, at least until her son (the later Edward VII) started going off the rails, and her beloved husband died in 1861. Luckily for everyone else, she immediately went into purdah, so as not to be too much of a misery. Outside the walls of her palaces, it all seemed immensely hopeful.

The Victorians should have enjoyed the moment. It was not to last. Even at the time, the 'Golden Years' were losing some of their gilt. There were a couple of little depressions at the beginning of them, for example, the most serious set off by a banking collapse, and a 'Great' one at the very end; and terrible working conditions for the working classes all through. Dickens's *Hard Times*, his most devastating (and least funny) anti-capitalist novel, came out in 1854, and things hardly improved after that. Possibly the most ominous events, however, were happening abroad. A new united Germany was flexing her muscles, under her 'Iron Chancellor', Count Otto von Bismarck. Germany wasn't seen as a threat yet; indeed, in the war she provoked with the French in 1870 the British generally sided with her against their old enemy; but she added a new and potentially dangerous counter in the game of international diplomacy.

However, the main foretastes of greater trouble came in the colonies. The Indian 'Mutiny' of 1857–8 was a terrible blow. But there were others: the second 'Opium War', a Maori war in New Zealand, the Jamaica rebellion and two or three engagements in southern Africa. The grand implication of all these events was that it was no longer going to be possible to secure Britain's commercial interests, and the strategic interests related to them, like protecting trade *routes*, simply informally. 'Free-trade imperialism' was turning into 'free trade enforced by conventional imperialism'. One of the problems with that was that it was likely to involve increased *expense*, for colonial administration probably, though that might be able to be paid for through taxes raised locally (at the risk of local protest); and military defence certainly. That could only come from the Treasury; in other words, taxation. This might not have been such a problem were it not for the fact that Britain's whole commercial philosophy and system until now had been underpinned by the idea that taxation was fundamentally inimical to commercial enterprise; so that taxing people to pay to secure the latter was akin to killing, or at least severely injuring the reproductive organs of, the goose that was laying the Golden Age eggs.

Looked at in this way the year 1850 – the year of Palmerston's notorious '*civis Britannicus sum*' boast – could be seen as the real high point of the British Empire, measured in terms of effective power and global freedom of action, rather than any of the later dates or periods that are often taken to be its zenith: the 1880s, 1900, 1920, even 1945, or *circa* 1870 (which used to be my chosen date). After that it was all downhill. The steps down the hill are marked by a number of colonial acquisitions popularly regarded as stages in the *rise* of the British Empire, which of course they were in an obvious way – the Empire reached its greatest territorial extent in 1920, with its new postwar mandated territories, and Ireland still in there, just – but not in any realistic sense. It was already quite near its last legs.

In fact every colonial war that Britain as a nation engaged in after 1850 was designed to defend what she regarded as her existing interests, rather than to extend them, even if that was the effect they had; and the best you could say of their benefits to Britain is that they succeeded in slowing her decline, to an extent. The 'Scramble for Africa' of the 1880s and 1890s, for example, was sparked by unprecedented competition for colonies from (mainly) France and Germany, which was thought to pose a military danger to Britain's existing colonies there, and an economic threat to the whole basis of her commerce if the 'winners' erected tariff barriers in their new acquisitions. Britain's main efforts in negotiating the 'Scramble', therefore, once she had secured her more direct interests, were aimed at exacting promises of free trade from whoever else won in west-central Africa, which she secured, on paper at least (it is the reason for what appears now to be the somewhat misleading christening of Leopold II's new acquisition as the 'Congo *Free* State'); and, apart from that, ensuring that no one threatened her short route to her oriental colonies, which passed through Egypt and skirted eastern Africa. Sometimes the motive there is difficult to credit: Uganda, for example, is a very long way from the Suez Canal; but Britain argued that it controlled one of the headwaters of the Nile, which fed Egypt, and if it were cut off at the source could ruin her protectorate there. OK, it was a long shot; but in the paranoid atmosphere of what is called the 'New' imperialism it could have seemed plausible. One of the reasons for Britain's wars against the independent 'Boer' republics of South Africa (1880–1, 1899–1902) was the threat the Boers were supposed to pose – especially when the German Kaiser foolishly stepped in to support them – to Britain's longer trade route around the Cape. In all these cases there were clearly other motives and causes involved: gold and diamonds, for example, in the Transvaal

Republic; humanitarian (against the Arab slave trade) in eastern Africa. But most of these actions can be regarded as defensive: either of existing direct economic interests, or of indirect ones.

In many ways the 'Scramble for Africa' should be seen as a Scramble to *avoid* Africa; to duck out of the responsibility of ruling these countries, that is, while at the same time preserving access to their markets. It was in connection with the 'Scramble' that Gladstone came out with that statement (in Parliament) that he actually welcomed Germany's participation – 'All I say is "God speed her!" She becomes our ally and partner in the execution of the great purposes of Providence for the advantage of mankind';[3] and it explains why giving the Congo to Leopold seemed such a spiffing idea. The point was that Leopold *wasn't* France or Germany or Britain. His country was small; and in any case he didn't represent Belgium, but only himself and his capitalist friends. And his bid for the Congo came with all kinds of grandiose humanitarian promises attached. (Henry Stanley, an anti-slaver as well as a rather brutal explorer, who backed him, seems to have been taken in by them.) So this seemed yet another example where private or semi-private enterprise could get governments, and especially mutually suspicious governments, off the hook.

The climax of the 'New' imperialism for Britain was the second South African or 'Boer' War, whose negative results were probably more important than the positive. This is despite the fact that she won it; but only after a long struggle against a numerically much smaller and more 'backward' (Dutch) foe, and at the expense of some concessions to the Boers which came to be of enormous significance later on. Before then, however, the shocking inefficiency of the British and colonial armies in the conflict sent tremors of alarm through the military classes. To be sure, the British army hadn't distinguished itself much in the Crimean War nearly fifty years previously, except in bone-headed bravery: the Charge of the Light Brigade; but all that was supposed to have been put right by military reforms carried out in the 1870s. What particularly shocked people in the early 1900s was the 'physical deterioration' of working-class men volunteering for the Boer War, mentioned already, and which was seen as ominous for Britain if she ever got involved in a real, that is European, fight. Clearly she had to be cautious about spreading her commitments much wider; and indeed the end of the Boer War saw a virtual cessation of expansionary imperialism by Britain. (When Colonel Francis Younghusband conquered Tibet for Britain in 1904, he was told to hand it back.) Even at the time the South African victory was not regarded as one to be particularly proud of, but more of an embarrassment and a warning.

The war's other negative repercussion was the opposition that it stimulated in Britain (as well as, needless to say, nearly every other European country), which gave rise eventually to a greater degree of disillusion, as well as the better-known 'jingoism', than any war had provoked for many decades. A distinctive feature of this opposition was its anti-capitalist element, however much of a motive for the war capitalism may or may not have been in reality; based on the prominent part played by Cecil Rhodes and his mining interests in bringing it on, including stirring up a battle between his company's private forces and the Transvaal Boers (the 'Jameson Raid' of 1895); which failed, but was never forgotten thereafter. In 1902 the Liberal economist J. A. Hobson 'invented' the 'capitalist' or 'surplus capital' theory of imperialism generally, in a book – *Imperialism: A Study* – which influenced Lenin, and has been one of the staples of the debate over Western imperialism to the present day. Indeed, this might be said to be the wretched South African War's main negative repercussion in Britain; aside, of course, from all the British soldiers (4,774) who died.

Thereafter there was almost no more 'imperialism', in the expansionist sense, before World War I. Britain had enough to cope with in the colonies she already had. Bengal in India was pretty much aflame, due to resentment of its 'partition' by the government (though that partition turned out to be preferred by the Indians eventually: it is the basis of the present-day Bangladesh); seeping into Britain itself in 1909 when Sir Curzon Wyllie, a British Indian official, was shot dead by an Indian student on the steps of the Imperial Institute in London. That was met by coercion at first, and then – as often happened in the British Empire – by concessions (the 'Morley–Minto reforms'). There was also trouble – riots, bombs, assassinations, strikes – in Ireland, Egypt, the West Indies, Nigeria, Kenya and Natal in South Africa: the last put down brutally by the local government, after Natal, in common with the other South African provinces, had been permitted its racist franchise, and consequently all-white government, as the Boers' price for stopping the fighting. Churchill once called Natal 'the hooligan of the British Empire';[4] but he could do nothing about it for fear of provoking the settlers to take up arms again. This was the other, and probably most unfortunate, repercussion of the South African war; and it vividly illustrates the weakness of the Empire at this time. Not only the Empire; for it should not be forgotten that Britain herself was wracked with problems during this immediately pre-Great War period, with the famous 'Great Labour Unrest', anarchist atrocities, Lordly rebellions and suffragettes chaining themselves to things. Despite the common image of an 'Edwardian summer', seen of course through the lens of the War, this was not a happy time.

Which made the Great War itself, when it came, doubly or trebly ominous for Britain; and is one of the things that make it unlikely that the British government ever wanted it or deliberately brought it on. One could possibly believe this of a more right-wing administration, full of people – many of them were imperialists – who thought the workers could well do with a 'bracing' war to discipline and toughen them, that it could give them the excuse to shoot down strikers and rioters (a contingency plan for this was actually prepared),[5] and that yes, they might get a few more colonies out of it; but not for this moderately progressive and not overtly expansionist 'Lib–Lab' one. That does not of course excuse Britain from some degree of responsibility for the War. Left-wing anti-imperialists had been warning for some years of a possible conflagration due to 'capitalist competition' among the major powers, in an extra-European market that was more or less all parcelled out now, leaving little room for expansion except at the expense of other capitalist–imperialist nations. That looked very plausible indeed in 1914. The main dispute between Britain and Germany before then was over German naval building, which was intended to bring the German Navy up to or very near the Royal Navy's establishment. Britain saw that as aggressive, because whereas she needed her navy to defend her far-flung empire, Germany had no such need. So Germany's naval building must have designs against Britain. Germany for her part – or her Kaiser, at least – was jealous of Britain's empire. So in a way the latter was at the bottom of it all; before the German invasion of Belgium, which Britain was treaty-bound to defend, brought a reluctant Empire in. (An 'empire' because George V technically declared war on behalf of the whole lot.)

In the end the British and French armies resisted effectively, until the USA later stepped in to help. Old imperialists, concerned about the lack of patriotism among the working classes in Britain under the pernicious influence of socialism, found they did not need to worry; most men were patriotic when it was a question of defending, not the Empire, but their country, homes and womenfolk. There were also of course the deterrents of imprisoning them if they refused 'conscription', introduced in 1916, or putting them in front of firing squads if they got cold feet under fire. So the British side won. So far as the Empire was concerned, that too seemed to hold up well. It all survived, albeit with more troubles in India, again met with concessions (the

Montagu–Chelmsford Declaration, 1917); in Ireland (the Easter Rebellion, here followed by repression); three-way (Arab–Jewish–British) conflict in Palestine; an Afrikaner rebellion in South Africa; and a great deal of discontent in Australia about how their brave soldiers had been led to the slaughter by idiot British officers at Gallipoli. British and colonial troops easily mopped up the new German colonies, which Germany by and large wasn't bothered with, and had a successful campaign against Germany's Ottoman allies in the Middle East, with the charismatic 'Lawrence of Arabia' purportedly galvanising the Arabs there. In the end Britain seemed to come out of the Great War stronger imperially than she had entered it, with the peace conferences granting her (together with France) a whole tranche of new colonial responsibilities, now called 'mandates', that is, held in trust for their peoples under the new League of Nations. If these are counted – as they should be: Britain claimed they were no different from her older colonies, which she also felt she had a kind of mandatory duty towards – they expanded the area of her imperial possessions to its greatest size ever. For extreme imperialists like Curzon and Milner – both co-opted into the war cabinet, incidentally – they seemed to fulfil their wettest dreams. Curzon in particular got a buffer zone for India stretching from the Mediterranean to Baluchistan. But virtually no one else at the time believed this expressed the reality.

Indeed, the interwar years were a period of almost continuous retreat, in various ways, all over the Empire, albeit disguised behind various façades that were designed to make it look more solid than it was. One of the most ingenious was the 'Commonwealth' ideal, mentioned already, which explained these events in terms of a transformation of the Empire, rather than a decline: its metamorphosis into what Britain had always intended it to be. That explained the grant of 'home rule' within the Empire to (most of) Ireland in 1921, for example; further reforms in India; more 'indirect rule' in Africa; giving the Middle East over to puppet rulers, but at least they were local and traditional ones; releasing the self-governing dominions from some irritating ties, like their lack of a say in war-declarations; and so on. At the same time, however, Britain was *coercing* her colonial subjects like crazy: shooting dead 400 unarmed Indian protestors in a closed square in Amritsar in the Punjab in 1919; bombing villagers in Palestine and Mesopotamia (Iraq) from airplanes, which even many of the RAF pilots involved felt was not cricket; setting the undisciplined and war-brutalised 'Black and Tans' against the IRA in Ireland; and other lesser (but still quite bloody) 'police' actions. For anti-imperialist historians this period stands out, together with the 1850s and '60s and then the 1950s and '60s, as one of the most 'atrocity'-filled; the inverted commas around 'atrocity', incidentally, not intended to imply that they weren't 'atrocious' in truth. (They mostly were.) Again, all of them were also strictly 'defensive'; though they may have been 'defending' the indefensible.

Just as in the early 1910s, and indeed as a continuation of some of the major trends in that tumultuous period, this was accompanied by domestic events that could also be regarded as dangerous to the Empire if you were that way inclined. Imperialists were always scared of working-class

socialism (as distinct from their own sort, 'social imperialism'), and tended to worry inordinately about, for example,
the General Strike of 1926, which even put the 'Great
Labour Unrest' in the shade; the election of two – albeit
minority – Labour governments; and the machinations of
communist spies and agents in their midst. Communists of
course – given a great boost by their recent successful revolution in Russia – were ideologically anti-imperial, having
picked up on Hobson, and were suspected of subverting
nationalist movements in the colonies too. This became
an obsession with Britain's new secret counter-subversive
agencies, especially MI5, recruited almost entirely from the
imperialist upper classes, right up until Stella Rimington
(Director General 1992–6). (Rimington had a sort of ex-
imperial connection; she had been recruited while working
for the diplomatic service in India.) MI5 gave the imperialists a new weapon to defend the Empire with: its own
means of subversion, which it – or perhaps MI6, or an even
more deeply hidden outfit – is supposed to have deployed
against the Labour government in 1924 (the 'Zinoviev
Letter' affair). But it was never likely to be enough. In reality
it seemed unlikely that the Empire would be able to survive
in its present form very much longer than the 1930s, and
it probably wouldn't have survived that long had it been
confronted by any convincing external enemies then. With
Germany taken out of the equation, Russia distracted by
its own internal post-revolutionary problems, and the USA
retreating into isolationism – refusing to join the League of
Nations, for example – Britain was given a relatively easy go
of it, apart from her own revolting colonial subjects. Again,

appearances were deceptive. Though the Empire still held together formally, and Britain looked to have retained its 'Great Power' status, it was largely on the sufferance of the world's two new potentially Greater Powers.

It was this realisation, and the perception – rightly as it turned out – that the Empire could not survive another big war, that led several prominent people on the imperial-ist Right of British politics to favour the 'appeasement' of Hitler in the 1930s, and has led some later historians to surmise that Britain might have held on to her empire had she kept out of World War II.[6] There were also other things going for that: Hitler's stand against Bolshevik Russia, for example, which made him a natural ally of the socialist-phobic British Right; and the offer he was supposed to have held out to Britain that he would let her keep all her colonies if she let him take all of continental Europe, so dividing the world between them.[7] Hitler, incidentally, was a great admirer of British India, and the 'ruthlessness' that had enabled Britain to keep hold of her, inculcated, he thought, in the public schools: 'calculated to rear men of inflexible will and ruthless energy who regard intellectual problems as a waste of time but know human nature and how to dominate other men in the most unscrupulous fashion';[8] which is not a testimonial you find much quoted nowadays. Fortunately (if you think that Nazism had to be put down) the old Harrovian Churchill, Britain's war leader from 1940, didn't go along with that; possibly because his brand of imperialism – and he was a terrific imperialist – was a very romantic kind, which believed that the colonies, even the dependent ones, were linked to Britain mainly through ties of affection and loyalty, rather than by 'unscrupulous domination'. That is essentially modelled on the feudal view of a lord's ideal relationship with his peasants. Churchill – 'the Great Commoner' – in fact came from a very old family. Sometimes upper-class naivety can be a boon.

The Second War, which of course Britain won, or rather Russia and the USA won for her, but only after a heroic defence for the first couple of years by Britain standing alone, spelt the end of the formal British Empire. Britain's hold on India just about snapped, which is why she went first; and loosened almost everywhere else. Again, as with previous periods of weakness, there were domestic reasons for its collapse then, including a third and *fairly* anti-imperialistic Labour government, this time with an overall majority; and virtual economic impoverishment, due to the war. This time the USA and the USSR were determined to play their parts in the disposition of the world after the conflict, with both, now, considering themselves to be anti-imperialist. (Of course, neither was.) Roosevelt, indeed, had insisted on Churchill's signing a joint declaration (the 'Atlantic Charter') of the 'right of all peoples to choose the form of government under which they will live' before he would commit America to the war effort, which Churchill tried to pretend only applied to Europe, but of course wasn't so easy to wriggle out of as that. Later, as we shall see, America adopted a slightly different attitude to the British Empire when she thought it might come in useful as a bastion against international communism; but that didn't last very long.

We have now come to the end of the history of the British Empire *effectively*. It formally collapsed in the twenty or thirty years after the end of World War II, as we shall see in the next chapter but one; though it could also be claimed that it had not been really viable since 1918, or 1902, or even 1850. Founded and initially built up at a time when Britain had a huge economic lead over the rest of the world, requiring free access to foreign markets, and based on a national ideology of 'liberalism' – easily the most dominant of her various 'discourses' – there was no way she could maintain it in a world as competitive and economically illiberal as it was increasingly becoming, without doing violence to her deepest beliefs; the kind of violence right-wing imperialists would have happily accepted, and most other imperial states, like Nazi Germany and Communist Russia, have adopted, but which would have required an entire upheaval of Britain's culture and institutions for her to accept. This is my reason for saying that, really, Britain's imperial decline went back to 1850. On the other hand it could also be said that, in another way, it was never completed at all, with quite a lot of residue still around. That idea will be pursued in the chapter after the 'decolonisation' one. Before that, we must explore the contentious issue of the effects of the Empire and imperialism on British society and culture; and vice versa.

SIX

The Empire at Home

T HE EMPIRE impacted on British society in a thousand different ways. Foodstuffs was one, with tea from
India and Ceylon, coffee from Kenya, sugar from the West
Indies, mutton from New Zealand and Australia and spices
from the East, to mention just the main ones. British gold
came from South Africa after the 1880s, cotton from India
and Egypt, rubber from Malaya, palm oil from West Africa,
and timber and beaver fur (for hats) from Canada. Worcester
sauce, despite its name, originated with an Indian recipe,
albeit adapted to the Briton's pallid taste. One imagines that
the opium ingested in Thomas De Quincey's literary circle
in the early nineteenth century, and found in a worrying
range of patent medicines afterwards, probably came from
India. More could be listed, but that would be tedious.

We need to get this into perspective. Britain always
imported more from other countries than she did from

the Empire. Until the later nineteenth century, most of her tea came from China, her timber from Russia and Finland, her coffee from Brazil, and the majority of her cotton – the staple of her industry and exports – from the USA. Coal was mined locally. Looking at what are supposed to be her favourite foods, eggs, bacon, roast beef, potatoes, fish and chips, and beer were all locally produced, and oranges for marmalade came from Spain. Haggises were bound to be from Scottish sheep's innards. In 1924 recipes for an 'Empire Christmas pudding' were given out, with all its ingredients Empire-sourced; but that was mainly as a propaganda effort, to show people what the Empire *could* provide. Posh people ate mainly French. No one (save returning ICS hands) ate curries, before the British left India. That was a post-colonial thing; as were Hunter Valley wines. Even when they were eating or using colonial products, people might not have realised it. Tea seems so English, after all. One bit of timber looks much like another. And Tate & Lyle never said a word on their packets about where and how their product was grown. As well as this, who is to say how much of what she bought from the colonies Britain would still have got if they had not been colonies, but independent countries? Not West Indian sugar, certainly; but probably much else. Trade and industry, and later banking and investment, were the keys to her prosperity, not formal empire per se. That at any rate is what nineteenth-century Liberals would have had you believe.

And then there were people. Emigration is the main link here between Britain and her empire; but even so, marginally more emigrants before the twentieth century ended up in the post-independence USA than in all the remaining colonies put together. Other sorts of traveller to the Empire were always greatly outnumbered by British visitors to the European continent. (That's explained mainly by the distances.) Europe also took a significant number of British emigrants, though they are rarely mentioned. A few of the upper middle classes went to the colonies as rulers or army officers, the aspirant middle classes as missionaries, working-class lads as soldiers, and odd bods as explorers. Traders traded there. The question is, however, how did all this impact on those who stayed behind? Emigrants sometimes began by writing letters back, if they could write at all, perhaps to encourage family to follow them (or to warn them off); but the correspondence usually ceased after a short while, leaving merely a temporary hole. Explorers and missionaries wrote stacks of books about their ripping adventures and good works among the benighted heathen, often presented as more benighted than they really were, for effect. Some of these were highly popular, among all classes, so far as we can tell. They also gave 'slide-shows'. Soldiers, if they survived – which was not at all guaranteed in the more unhealthy or hostile colonies – returned home generally to indifference or ignominy. (Ordinary squaddies weren't much respected in Victorian society.) Officers and rulers lived in their own genteel ghettos when they returned home, surrounded by assegais and little yellow gods, souvenirs of their glory days. It was they who mainly frequented the only Indian eating place in nineteenth-century London, the Hindostanee Coffee House in Portman Square, opened, by one Dean Mahomet from Patna, 'for the nobility and gentry'. There were very few immigrants *from* the dependencies in Britain: black and brown ones, that is. Even Australian cricket teams (apart from an 'Aboriginal' one in 1868, mainly regarded as a curiosity, though it played very well) didn't start coming over until 1880. The 'empire strikes back' phenomenon was something that took a while to get under way.

But this of course is a very pedantic way of looking at it. It doesn't take account of the *quality* of the experience that the Empire brought home. There may only have been one 'Hindostanee Coffee House', but it must have stood out as exotic, in those dull London streets. Brighton's Indo-Saracenic Royal Pavilion, begun in 1787 for the Prince Regent, was a similarly rare example of orientalism in English architecture, but obviously impressed people – as it still does. At a very much lower artistic – and moral – level were some infamous travelling 'exhibitions' of 'native races' around the middle of the nineteenth century, the exhibits dressed either in weird and wonderful costumes, or scarcely any costumes at all, dancing and grimacing: there were not all that many of them, as it happens; but even if you only saw one it must have left a mark. From the 1880s through to the 1920s there was a series of much greater exhibitions to show the wonders of the Empire off to the people, the biggest, in 1924, bequeathing England's national football stadium to the nation, approached along the 'Empire Way', to remind people of its origin long after the event. Doubts were expressed at the time over whether the message of these shows was really getting through, especially to young visitors: 'I've brought you here to see the wonders of the Empire', says one of Noël Coward's characters, 'and all you want to do is go on the dodgems';[1] but this is just anecdotal, and it is difficult to imagine some of the patina not rubbing off.

Other visual reminders of the Empire included nine-teenth-century 'diorama' shows (huge moving illustrated backcloths on rollers), some twentieth-century feature films, paintings of battles, the occasional march-past of colonial soldiers through London at royal jubilees, coronations and funerals; and even some Empire-themed advertising post-ers: an African fleeing from a lion on a Raleigh bicycle; Pears soap being used on a little black boy; 'Smoke Empire Tobacco', and so on. Juvenile literature is another field which took to the Empire in quite a big way, albeit written by men (and one or two women) who felt an obligation to 'imperialise' youth by this means – weaning them off the 'penny dreadfuls' which seemed to be their favourite read-ing otherwise. Again, as with food, we have to put these into perspective. Firstly, most of the overt imperial visual propaganda only appeared after around 1880, at the earliest. We must be careful not to read back from there. Secondly, there were always far more non-imperial restaurants, pavil-ions, dioramas, exhibitions (the 1851 'Great' Exhibition was one), march-pasts, children's stories and the rest than 'Empire' ones; and even among 'exoticisms' the Empire found it hard to compete with continental Europe and America, or Britain's own history, for the people's interest: medievalism, for example (the Gothic Revival), and the 'Western' genre in cinemas. But of course people could be interested in and thrilled by all these. And even overtly non-imperial cultural productions could be peppered with imperial allusions.

The issue remains, did this really indicate much of a specifically imperial interest or enthusiasm among the general population of Britain, as opposed to a merely 'exotic' one? One obvious problem lies in the fact that so much of it was *propaganda*; which begs two questions: firstly, why did imperialists feel they needed to put so much effort into it if their compatriots were reliably imperialistic in any case; and secondly, how can we tell whether their propaganda really had the effect they intended? To come anywhere near close to answers to these questions we need to approach them tangentially. Who were the people the propaganda was aimed at? What were the conditions in which they lived, their basic interests, their experience of life, the intellectual environment they inhabited, the other influences working on them, the state of their knowledge outside the propaganda they were subjected to, and their relationship to the propagandists themselves? Bearing all this in mind – the 'demand' part of the equation – how *likely* were they to have been won over? Of course, if one regards people, or at least the working classes, who were the propagandists' main targets, as merely empty vessels, whose minds would receive anything poured into them, the answer is simple. We can't – in the interests of another kind of open-mindedness – rule this out. But it is a more patronising and insulting assumption than most of us, probably, would prefer to make. (Contemporary imperialists certainly didn't.) For that reason, we really need to look into all the other possibilities.

One of the motives for the propaganda was to inculcate an imperial patriotism, which, as well as favouring imperial-*ism*, would also unite the different classes of Britain together in a way very little else quite seemed to do. Exceptions were people's pride in their 'freedoms'; xenophobia, generally against continental Europeans (especially the French); and of course Britain's wars. 'Freedom', however, was a vague concept, interpretable in various ways, some of which the imperial classes might not like; and the other two were merely negative. The basic problem was that British people's sense of national identity was often overridden by their class, religious or other kinds of identity, which could threaten social stability. This was very much the situation in Edwardian times, culminating in the 'Great Labour Unrest', which also happened to be a high point of imperial propaganda. It could be that the achievement of social stability, and especially industrial peace, was a major motivation for imperial propagandists at this time, which is not to say, however, that they were not genuine in their 'imperialism' too. National unity through patri-otism, of any kind, was an unfamiliar idea throughout most of the eighteenth and nineteenth centuries, when the classes were supposed to be bound together not by anything they had in common, but by the *links* that bound them, usually in terms of mutual obligations: the workers worked for the upper classes, who looked after the workers, and so on. That was the 'feudal' part of the British hybrid, still operating; though easily adaptable to middle-class – employer–employee – relationships too. It mostly worked. But a result of it was a peculiar resistance to 'patriotism' in Britain as a whole; though there were patriotism*s*, attached to each different class. Thus, the upper-class view of a 'Briton' contrasted sharply with the radical working-class view; indeed, for the latter English- or Britishness was defined in apposition to the former – Anglo-Saxons and Celts against Normans. (Hence Dr Johnson's famous attack on 'patriotism': 'the last refuge of the scoundrel'.) This was a difficult barrier to break down.

It was, however, only after the 1880s that this became a serious problem. It is important to emphasise, in order to explain the quite sudden appearance of imperialist propaganda around then, that public support for imperialism had not been *needed* before. This was for two reasons. Firstly, hardly anyone had the vote, so the majority of people could be ignored. Secondly, the Empire didn't cost much, in money or men, apart from army volunteers, so it didn't touch even voters where it mattered most to them. Sometimes people wonder how Britain could have accumulated and run a vast empire if her people were largely indifferent to it; this is the answer. It is another reason for doubting the ubiquity of imperial sentiment in the early- and mid-Victorian years – if it wasn't *required*. Later, however, things changed. From the 1870s onwards, international imperialism started getting truly competitive; at the same time as more and more Britons were being taken into the body political. (Two Reform Acts, of 1867 and 1884–5, quadrupled the electorate.) It was then that, for almost the first time in the nineteenth century, it was thought that a truly *national* effort would be needed to secure the Empire. That meant that the plebs would have to be taken on board.

Whether imperial propaganda could do it was questionable. The idea, of course, was to identify all Britons with the imperial cause. But some propagandists chose problematical ways of doing this; like one who sought to inspire the working classes by asking them to compare themselves to the bases or plinths on which statues of imperial heroes stood.[2] You couldn't get rid of the feudal. The result was that each class retained its own, separate value system, which was likely to respond to imperial propaganda in different ways. For the propagandists, this was not helped by their education, which (as J. R. Seeley noted in the 1880s) neglected the Empire shamefully, certainly in the nineteenth century.[3] The public schools taught almost no imperial history at all, except Roman, which may have served as a proxy for the British. Middle-class school history syllabuses concentrated on the 'growth of [domestic] liberty' theme. Working-class education, such as it was, saw no place for any subject beyond training pupils in their utilitarian duties to the middles and uppers. Some were discouraged from learning geography, outside the borders of their home villages, so there was no hope for Africa or India. Informing this was often a fear of their getting 'above themselves'. In particular, their masters were chary of their learning any colonial history, in case they started empathising with the colonised. Of course, there existed a few school textbooks on imperial history, from the 1890s onwards; but written more in hope that the system might change, than to fulfil a demand. (One of them, C. L. R. Fletcher and Rudyard

Kipling's *A School History of England*, 1911, was roundly mocked at the time for its rampant jingoism, and was probably only 'set' in private 'prep' schools.) Another problem was that many elementary school teachers were working class themselves (it was another of those occupations, like missionary work, that attracted class aspirers; my father was one), and were unimpressed by imperialism, to say the least. They largely resisted Lord Meath's idea of an 'Empire Day' holiday for schools, for example, until 1916. (Canada and Australia took to it much earlier.) Even when it was imposed on them (by local councils) it was treated *only* as a holiday, with very little patriotic content. Of course, there were many exceptions. And education doesn't only come in classrooms. In their playgrounds kids used to play 'Britons and Boers' at the turn of the century – as an alternative to 'Cowboys and Indians'. And then there were all those 'ripping yarns'; though there is some – again anecdotal – evidence that little of the overt imperialism in these rubbed off. There was also Baden-Powell's Boy Scout movement after 1908, originally with a deliberate imperial agenda; but the evidence suggests that it never caught on with poorer boys – Baden-Powell's main target – who used to yell insults at the bewoggled scouts as they marched by. As for the others, it was mainly the camping that attracted them. Overall the evidence that nineteenth- and early-twentieth-century working-class youngsters were ripe for imperial indoctrination is mixed at best, and at worst very thin. Which of course might help explain why the imperialists felt they had to work so hard on them, and were never happy with the results.

When the children grew up – and indeed before then – they were subjected to other influences which countered the imperial one to an extent, or at least worked to modify it. Socialism and trade unionism were two, despite the imperialists' attempts to capture those two ideologies, for example with 'social imperialism' and a 'Trade Union Tariff Reform Association', which were never felt to match up to the real things. It would take a lot to lure the working classes away from their natural antipathy to their employers. Whatever the degree of 'imperialisation' they underwent in the nineteenth and twentieth centuries, the imperialists themselves never thought it was anywhere near enough. They were particularly unimpressed by the occasional outbreak of working-class 'jingoism', for example, like the famous riots on 'Mafeking Night' in May 1900 (following the 'relief' of that town), which they regarded as merely superficial, more akin to hooliganism than to genuine imperialism – they were almost certainly right about this – and as such a potential threat to them. (Of course, the Right typically exaggerates these things.) There were other adverse ideological factors too; like *some* sections of Nonconformist Christianity, strong among the upper working and lower middle classes, which was closely allied to old-fashioned liberalism and pacifism, and so tended to be anti-imperialist. (For a short time the Wesleyans went the other way.) What may be more significant, however, is the type of imperialism that even the imperialists among these people – workers, lower middle classes, socialists, Methodists – espoused when they did. It was never the aggressive or authoritarian kind that the upper-class imperialists seemed happier with. It had to be consistent with their older and deeper class discourses; and the 'libertarian' one in particular. After World War I, they found the 'Commonwealth' idea almost tailor-made for them.

All this also explains why the Empire was not as prominent in the *culture* of the time as we might expect – that is, 'culture' defined in any way we wish. Again, it is possible to cherry-pick exceptions: Kipling, of course, and one or two lesser poets; juvenile literature (not usually adult, unless it was critical); one or two of Elgar's weaker musical works, and some more by Arthur Sullivan; Edwardian neo-Roman buildings; the battle paintings of Lady Elizabeth Butler; G. F. Watts's equestrian statue *Physical Energy*, inspired by Cecil Rhodes; some bits of 'orientalism': all this among the 'high' – or highish – art of the time. Lower down, the music hall was famous for popular jingoism, enough to alarm the Left about the allegiance of the working classes: J. A. Hobson, for example, who wrote about it; but then the Left tends to exaggerate, too. Most of the popular press was owned by rich imperialists, and was notorious even at that time for exaggerating the villainies of Britain's imperial enemies, and making things up. (The *Daily Mail* was a particular offender here. Its correspondent in South Africa was actually a 'pro-Boer', but filed anti-Boer articles in deference to his proprietor.[4]) Again, what can one tell from this? Music-hall songs are much more likely to have been popular because of their tunes than the words; and in any case the great majority of them were *not* patriotic.

(Poverty, drink, policemen and romantic love were the commonest themes.) There are almost no imperial theatre plays. Representations of the Empire in the 'fine' arts are surprisingly sparse, partly due to arty-crafty people's disdain for 'masculine' pursuits. (Despite her title, Lady Elizabeth Butler was very much looked down on by the aesthetic set.) It is for this kind of reason that we cannot make any more general deductions from works of art about the 'popularity' of the Empire at the time. In most cases, there were special factors operating, which may make them unrepresentative. Art does *not* necessarily reflect life, and should not be assumed to, without a great deal of historical context and adjustment.

In fact, artistic and intellectual life in Britain in the last years of the nineteenth century and the first of the twentieth was astonishingly rich, lively, original and above all *variegated*. Maybe there is a way in which that reflects Britain's imperial dynamism at this time; but it is not a direct or obvious one. It would strain relevance – and stretch my own expertise – to attempt to survey all the wonderful things that were going on in Britain then largely outside of and unaffected by 'imperialism': Wilde, Whistler, Mackintosh, Voysey, Pater, Burne-Jones, Beardsley, Hardy, Morris, Conrad (apart from the ambivalent *Heart of Darkness*), Conan Doyle, Galsworthy, Chesterton, Swinburne, Wells... (I'm sorry if I've missed out anyone's favourite); beyond pointing out that it *was* a highly diverse cultural environment, with so many different 'discourses' operating at the same time as to make it impossible to pick a 'dominant' one. It was the same in politics, with a far broader palette of possible ideologies doing the rounds than today, from free-market anarchism at one extreme, through more conventional brands of liberalism and conservatism, morphing into authoritarianism, then state socialism, through to anarcho-socialism – where of course it joined up with free marketism again. (Political beliefs should be seen as a circle, rather than a scale with 'poles'.) All these ideas were taken seriously and openly discussed in respectable political circles and journals, with none of them being regarded, unlike today, as beyond the pale. 'Imperialism' was one – or rather, several – of these, coming somewhere between authoritarianism and state socialism. By the same token, so was anti-imperialism.

We have discussed already why 'anti-imperialism' was such a weak plant before the end of the nineteenth century. It wasn't because people were necessarily *pro*-imperialist. There were problems with the word, with Britons unaware that it could be applied to what they were doing in the world; secondly, it was more difficult to conceive of an alternative to 'imperialism' in an age before nationalities; and thirdly, there seemed to be far more constructive alternatives available to the kinds of imperialism that did run naturally against most middle- and working-class political values, and might even be seen as more anti-imperialist in reality: for example, protecting weak peoples against other worse imperialisms – slaving, say, or capitalist. All the ingredients were there for a genuine anti-imperialism if it were ever called for: the powerful liberal and 'progressive' discourses of the day, unless you were so confident of these that you felt entitled to impose them on other peoples; anti-militarism; anti-authoritarianism or even anti-government; isolationism; anti-exploitation; anti-spending; justice; toleration; solidarity; and being nice to people – not necessarily all together under the same skins, of course. What eventually pulled some of these together in a coherent 'anti-imperial' ideology were the dramatic imperial events of the very end of the nineteenth century: the South African war above all, but before that events in Egypt, the Sudan and China. At first it was a traditional Liberal, Cobdenite reaction; but then it took on the anti-capitalist element that has distinguished it since. That was because of the very obvious part played by 'capital' in many of these events. The man credited with dreaming up the 'theory' of capitalist imperialism was J. A. Hobson, deriving it not from socialism (though the socialists had got almost all the way there before him), but from his belief that free trade, which he supported, had been diverted from its true path by *monopoly* capital. That is why he remained a Liberal; or a 'bourgeois', as Lenin dismissively called him after pinching the idea.

Whether the nuances of his theory were truly grasped by everyone, it chimed in with many people's impatience with a form of capitalism which by that time (the early twentieth century) had become pushy and vulgar, and had wandered very far indeed from its egalitarian roots. (Mr Toad in *The Wind in the Willows* was an exemplar.) It was also associated with Jews; hence the anti-Semitic ring to some – but only some – of the anti-imperialism of the time. This, however, didn't necessarily make the anti-capitalists 'anti-imperialists' *tout court*, for reasons already mentioned here. Even Hobson wasn't. This has been taken to indicate that even so-called 'antis', and therefore all Britons, were imperialists *really*, having soaked up the 'dominant discourse' of the age, whether they realised it or not.[5] But there was a good and rational reason for not going the whole hog over this, which we should be more than ever aware of today: which was that the removal of formal – that is, state – imperial control over other countries didn't necessary liberate them from imperialisms of other kinds. In Hobson's time it was the predations of European, Middle Eastern and Asian rivals, who would be bound to leap in to fill the vacuum left by any retreating empire; and also – running on from his 'capitalist theory' – unchecked exploitation by international capitalist companies. (We have seen that, whatever its other failings, the British Empire did, albeit only very occasionally, seek to hold these back.) So there was, and is, a problem here. Simply abandoning your colonies was no solution; it smacked of irresponsibility. Hobson's answer, eventually, was to *internationalise* the practice of empire by giving it over to a world body to administer, in the world's rather than individual nations' interests. He was looking forward here, of course, to the postwar League of Nations and its 'Mandates Commission', of which he was one of the ideological begetters.

That could be said to be a form of imperialism too, of course; and the very idea of 'responsibility' has a plangent imperial ring. In that case there was probably no getting away from it, and it was unreasonable to expect Britons to, even if all the instincts of many of them, and their underlying values, pointed that way. The most we can expect of them is that they were critical of the imperialism of the time, which many of them were. They became even more so when they realised what competitive international imperialism was leading to (as they saw it) in the ominous years before World War I. By the end of that war, as we shall see in the next chapter, the only sort of 'imperialism' that was acceptable to most of them was the gentler, protective, preparing-for-self-government sort that was represented by the new 'Commonwealth' ideal. That's because it could be squared with the deeper, liberal discourse that had always been dominant over, or at least a close challenger to, the 'imperialist' one in middle- and working-class Britain from the eighteenth century on.

It was this that marked domestic British society off from colonial British ones. Britons at home and Britons abroad started (obviously) from the same place. But then they diverged. Local circumstances, together with what I have called their 'functions', either confirmed or modified their attitudes. Stay-at-home Britons were not subjected to the same influences as their colonial cousins, and so were more likely to retain the liberal values most of them were brought up with; depending on the situation in Britain alone. Because the Empire was not all around them, in the obvious way it was with the colonials, it was unlikely to affect them so much. It may be significant that, while Lord Meath's 'Empire Day' was being resisted in Britain, it was avidly embraced in Canada, Australia and New Zealand, in the first of these cases as early as 1904. A lesson from this is not to infer the imperial attitudes of people in Britain from those of their compatriots abroad. They were different. (The ones who gave Edward Said his first experience of Englishmen, in Egypt, seem to have been a bit mad.) Which is why, as has been remarked before, so many of the latter felt so unsettled if and when they returned 'home'.

One other possibility, sometimes mooted, is that the British had to be instinctive imperialists because of their attitudes to 'race'. The idea here seems to be that because they regarded 'non-white' peoples as inferior, they felt it gave them a right to annex and rule them. There is indeed plenty of evidence of casual racism in British society throughout the imperial period; and from about the middle of the nineteenth century of some proper 'scientific' racist theories emerging. Those exhibitions of 'natives' travelling the country undoubtedly encouraged the former, which was mirrored in children's books, comics, cartoons, art, even music (John Pridham's *Abyssinian Expedition*, with its 'Ethiopian Song', the words of which are 'Yah ha yah ha yah ha'), and a dozen other forms. This sort of thing is, of course, not peculiar to Britain, and may not have been more pronounced or widespread there because of her imperial links. Nineteenth-century Swedish school textbooks, for example, are more consistently – and certainly more 'scientifically' – 'racist' than Britain's.[6] British domestic views of other races at that time were almost never based on personal contact or observation, as they became, of course, when the substantial immigration of black and brown people started in the 1950s. (In the nineteenth century there had been some, but very localised, usually in port cities. The immigration 'problem' then centred around Irish, European political refugees, and Jews.) Without a large population of non-whites to test it, there is no saying what the whites' practical relationship with them would have been. Comic-book images might have faded. The most likely scenario is that people's attitudes would have varied with the type of contact they had with them, as they did between 'whites' and 'blacks' out in the colonies. Lastly, there is no reason to believe that British imperialism was significantly *motivated* by race prejudice, over many other, more material causes.

In fact many who were racists were anti-imperialist for that reason: because they believed that other races were so inferior that there was no point in colonising them. You could take that position even if you were a liberal in other ways, as Charles Dickens was: deriding Britain's 'humanitarian' mission abroad because the Africans, Indians and the rest were simply not up to it. Besides, charity began at home. Another anti-imperialist racist was the Frenchman Count Gobineau, who opposed his country's colonial expansion on the grounds that it might threaten the 'purity' of the white race (those seductive oriental women). In other words – though these are only two examples – imperialism and racism are not inextricably bound together. If you could be a racist without being an imperialist, you could certainly be a non-racist imperialist too. It depended what you wanted to do with the other races. And in Britain itself there was nothing you could do with them (until 1950), because there were hardly any there. Looking outside, there is quite a lot of evidence that home-based Britons generally deplored the overtly racist policies that the Afrikaners pursued in South Africa; indeed, it was one of their 'excuses' (though no more than that) for provoking the Boer War. When the eventual settlement of that war, the Treaty of Vereeniging (1902), permitted the newly conquered Afrikaner republics to continue their discrimination, just about everyone in the British House of Commons, on both sides, deplored that as a necessity, at best. (Otherwise the Boers wouldn't settle.) Some of them hoped that 'liberal progress' – which they mostly had great faith in – would bring the racists to their senses eventually. In the meantime, however, they registered their disapproval.

But who can know what was in anybody's mind at these times? There were undoubtedly Britons whose hearts swelled at the thought of all the glory and, they thought, power that the great British Empire represented; who thrilled at reports of their brave redcoats taming the savage (when they managed to); who believed that British ideas, of politics, religion, culture and all the rest, were the best that had ever been thought of, and so applicable to everyone in the world: who were, in other words, full-blown imperialists of one kind or another. There were also many who didn't share this arrogance and vainglory; sympathised with the 'natives', either empathetically or patronisingly; were highly discomforted by atrocities in the colonies, when the impe-rialist press deigned to report them; and were deeply uneasy about the role that international capital – mistrusted even if you were an old-fashioned liberal free trader – seemed to be playing in all this.

It is in fact impossible to tell from the 'evidence' we have available what the British (at home) thought of the empire their rulers were acquiring for them. 'Mafeking Night' was of course not a reliable indication. Nor may be their apparent indifference towards most other imperial events. We have no true tests of opinion on these matters: no 'Gallup polls' before World War II, for example, and not even any dependable parliamentary votes. (The issues here were usually clouded.) The best we can do is to theorise: on the basis of hypotheses about human nature and psychology, especially people's suggestibility (for example, to propaganda); on the nature of colonialism; and on the ubiquity of 'dominant discourses' generally – or whatever. Then, however, we need to *test* these hypotheses against what evidence there is, sensitively, to take account of the ambiguity of that evidence; and in as much *context* as possible. In this particular case it will not tell us whether the British people were 'imperialistic' or not; but it might help to narrow down – or extend – the possibilities.

What we can say is this. Firstly, imperialism was not *driven* by popular feeling. There is no evidence at all of that; of parliamentary elections, for example, being affected one way or another by imperial issues, except in the heat of war (1900 is probably the only example); or of pro-imperial sentiment among 'ordinary' people existing independently and in advance of the top-down propaganda designed to stir it up. So popular imperialism, insofar as it existed, was not *responsible* for the reality of imperialism in any way at all. Secondly, the Empire certainly impacted on Britons and on British society materially, but not exclusively, and not in a way that the British were necessarily conscious of. If they were conscious of it they didn't necessarily have strong opinions about it, one way or another, as it very rarely made any direct demands on them, and it wasn't important to their political rulers that they should have positive opinions about it, in order for example to inculcate 'patriotism'. That was before the 1880s. After then imperialists began seeing what *they* regarded as people's *indifference* to the Empire as a danger, which they therefore sought to correct by means of propaganda. How effective that propaganda was is impossible to say, though it may be significant that imperialists never felt confident enough of its impact to let up. The reason for this is that it was clear to them – as it should be to us – that British politics and culture comprised a jumble of different ideas, value systems and 'discourses' at that time, none of which can be said to be 'dominant' (unless it was 'liberal progress'), which therefore the imperial discourse had either to fight against, or else to adapt to. The myth of a 'liberal' empire that was created around the time of World War I – the 'Commonwealth' – was a clever way of doing the latter; acknowledging as it did the probable primacy of the 'liberal' discourse in Britain over the 'imperial' one. And it worked in stemming root and branch anti-imperialism for a while.

SEVEN

The Beginning
of the End

ALL EMPIRES probably contain within themselves the
seeds of their own destruction; which should mean
that really the beginning of the British Empire's end came
at its start. There is certainly a sense in which this could
be said to be true, with its initial expansion taking place
in conditions that could not possibly be sustained, and
its later expansion being in effect a way of trying to cope
with the implications of this. In an earlier chapter I put
the high point of Britain's imperial sway at around 1850,
after which further annexations of territory, coupled a little
later on with the encouragement of a positive imperialistic
ideology, were undertaken mainly in order to put a brake
on its downward trajectory. These failed, however, as they
were bound to; and as the years between the two world wars
made increasingly obvious to all but the most blinkered
imperialists – of whom, however, there were quite a few.

The latter could perhaps be forgiven in the immediate aftermath of World War I, from which Britain had emerged on the winning side, and with the whole of her empire seemingly intact. Indeed, it had even made some gains, in the form of the ex-German and ex-Ottoman colonies 'mandated' to her by the treaties of Versailles and Sèvres in 1919–20. In strictly literal terms, that was the date of its maximum territorial extent; Britain's imperial zenith, therefore, in a way. One could argue that the 'Mandates' shouldn't be counted, as they were merely held 'in trust' for the League of Nations; but most people regarded that as a fig leaf: 'the crudity of conquest,' as the historian H. A. L. Fisher put it, 'draped in the veil of morality';[1] and for its part the British government professed not to be able to tell the difference either: for weren't *all* her colonies also held 'in trust' in a way? But in any case it wasn't long before the impression of *imperial* victory came to seem somewhat tarnished, with colonial rebellions that had been bubbling beneath the surface during the war bursting into the open, and at least two of the new 'Mandates' – Palestine and Mesopotamia – proving far more trouble than they were worth. These, together with domestic crises, growing 'anti-imperialism' in Britain, discontent in the army that was supposed to police all these possessions, and the looming presence of two potential 'superpowers' on both western and eastern horizons, made the interwar period a critical one for the British Empire.

Again, it stumbled through; repressing here, conceding there, refurbishing its 'image' really quite cleverly, and fortunate in the disposition of the world around it, with neither the non-imperialist USA nor the anti-imperialist USSR (if you took their own pretensions at face value) pulling their full weights against it; until the outbreak of Hitler's war, which many on the British political Right feared would mark the end of their empire: which is exactly what it did. It started with India, liberated in 1947, in two pieces, later to become three: present-day India, Pakistan and Bangladesh; followed by Burma, Ceylon and Palestine in 1948 – the last given over to an intermittent civil war between Arabs and Jewish colonialists: not Britain's finest moment; and then, in the 1950s and '60s, a whole tranche of colonies in Africa, South East Asia, the Pacific, the Mediterranean and the Caribbean. By that time most British politicians, including liberal Conservatives like Harold Macmillan, had come to read the auguries accurately – viz. Macmillan's famous 1960 'wind of change' speech in Cape Town;[2] leading them to re-gird their loins to secure a dignified end to the Empire, rather than trying to prop it up. This, after all, would be how the British Empire would be remembered in history: not only for what it was while it lived, but for the manner of its death.

They already had a kind of template for that, in the form of the long tradition in British imperial history of 'trusteeship', thin though that line appeared at times, and occasionally hypocritical: deployed simply to appease the liberal discourse in British society. According to at least one version of this ideology, the whole purpose of British imperialism was to prepare or 'raise' its subjects to a level from which they could take the reins of their own governments, which transformed 'decolonisation' into the climax of the whole business, rather than a failure of any kind. People at home were already prepared for this by the 'Commonwealth' scenario; and possibly by the visits of Indian and West Indian cricket teams between the wars, playing 'Tests' against England on (literally) level playing fields. If you could bat and bowl a bit, and without a white man to set your field for you, it really helped. Cricket is a sophisticated game, after all. This is largely how the Commonwealth is pictured today. It was a valuable way of seeming to avoid the dreaded 'decline and fall' scenario so familiar to classically trained public schoolboys. The Empire didn't fall, it simply metamorphosed. And the continued existence of the Commonwealth – joined immediately and voluntarily by newly independent India, and then by most of the other ex-colonies – was testimony to that.

Alas, it wasn't in fact quite like that. Britain's decolonisation was painted at the time and in some retrospective accounts as a mainly smooth and friendly process, with self-government being 'granted' to her ex-colonies when they were ready for it, unlike in the case of France – she was the usual comparator – where the process was far more violent and painful; but comparing the two 'decolonisations' overall there really is very little to choose between them. In nearly every British case independence was not 'granted', but had to be conceded after bitter struggles against powerful nationalist oppositions, and against a background of international – mainly Soviet, US and UN – antipathy to imperialism that was irresistible. Indian independence was rushed through at a time of terrible communal violence between Hindus and Muslims; some of that possibly due to the imminent removal of Britain's protective role. In Palestine, Britain never achieved the multicultural solution that, in her idealistic way, she saw as the best one for both Arabs and Jews. Tories called these 'scuttles', and they were. Other colonies suffered from similar problems: internal racial, cultural and religious divisions; with similar bloody outcomes when they were left to themselves. In some cases, Nigeria and Sudan for example, these lasted for decades. Many African colonies' 'preparations' for self-government – setting up native civil services and local democracies, pushing economic development, and so on – began so very tardily that they were nowhere near ready when native nationalists forced the hand of the British government; usually because they had been starved of means for years, and because of the complacent assumptions of the amiable but bone-headed 'men on the spot' that they had decades, even centuries, ahead of them yet. One colonial nationalist leader, Hastings Banda of Nyasaland, actually pleaded with the colonial government in 1951 to keep hold of his country until it was better prepared.[3] In that case it was to keep it out of the hands of the neighbouring 'Rhodesias', which were plotting to incorporate it into a settler-dominated federation. This was the other fly – or huge great wasp – in the ointment: white *settlers*, who were the ones who delayed Zimbabwe's independence with majority rule until 1980, and caused all kinds of troubles in Kenya. It was the privateers, again.

In (Southern) Rhodesia, Britain had contracted her responsibility out to them long before, and indeed never properly 'ruled' the country at any time in its history, since Cecil Rhodes's British South Africa Company had bought it up and then exploited it in his own capitalist – and also imperialist, for he was a genuine one of those – interests in the 1890s. Britain had a governor there, but his role was effectively little more than that of an ambassador or consul in a foreign country, simply reporting back to the Colonial Office what was going on. White Rhodesians always assumed that when self-government was granted it would be to *them*, as it had been in Britain's other dominions, including their near neighbour the Union (later Republic) of South Africa. Britain was still the titular ruler of their country, however, and was being pressured by international as well as a large slice of domestic opinion, and the Rhodesian Africans (though the white Rhodesians disputed this; they claimed it was just 'agitators'), only to devolve power to the majority there. Successive governments attempted to broker compromises, but failed. In the end, in 1965, the white Rhodesian minority issued a 'Unilateral Declaration of Independence', which could, in international law, have been met by military force by Britain, but the then Labour government reckoned it couldn't risk such action in case British soldiers refused to fight other white men. (This had been a problem in the American War of Independence, too.) The end result was a fifteen-year period of attrition and bloody civil war in Rhodesia, resulting in the whites' enforced surrender. That was anything but smooth and friendly; and the aftermath hardly a tribute to Britain's way of going about these things.

To the north, Kenya, if anything, fared worse. The underlying problem there, again, was a settler population – smaller, and reputedly more posh and morally corrupt than elsewhere (though that may have been an exaggeration) – together with a smaller Asian one and a much larger African one, governed this time by proper colonial officials, and wanting at the very least a 'multi-racial' form of self-government, with guaranteed representation for them, the settlers; but faced with huge resentment and ultimately a savage rebellion by the natives – mainly Kikuyu – whose best lands the whites had appropriated in the recent past. In that case Britain did send in forces, but against the Kikuyu ('Mau Mau'), with terrible effects: atrocities on both sides, but particularly stomach-turning on the part of the authorities, the scale of whose judicial killings and the sheer obscenity of whose tortures (hot eggs pushed into vaginas, for example) certainly exceeded those of the Americans fifty years later in Abu Ghraib. One interesting feature of this is the way it was 'covered up' afterwards; firstly by the new president of independent Kenya, Jomo Kenyatta, who was embarrassed by some of Mau Mau's excesses and wanted to set out with a clean sheet; and by the British, who hid most of the records of these events away in a hidey-hole in Buckinghamshire until they were discovered in the early 2000s by a couple of historical researchers, and lawyers working on behalf of old Kenyan victims who wanted to take the current British government to court.[4] We shall return to this in the final chapter. It makes any account of

Britain's decolonisation history, like this one, fundamentally unreliable, until the government comes clean.

Britain's troops were involved in fighting elsewhere too: Cyprus, Malaysia, Aden, Northern Ireland (if that is still counted as a colony); and her secret services deeply implicated both in these colonies, and elsewhere in the world where British interests were thought to be at stake: Egypt, Iran, the Congo and elsewhere. MI6 tried to assassinate President Nasser of Egypt, for example; was involved in the plot that removed Mohammad Mosaddeq from Iran in 1953; and *may* have been partly responsible for the toppling of prime minister Patrice Lumumba of the Congo in 1961. The truth of many of these events is not fully known yet, and may never be. But enough is known, surely, to scotch the idea that in Britain's case the process of decolonisation was the friendly, voluntary and civilised affair it has often been taken to be.

Nor was it *complete*. When Britain surrendered her colonies, she didn't give up everything. This was what most of the struggles with the nationalists were about: not whether Britain could hold on to their territories, which she had more or less given up on anyway by the 1950s, but whether their 'free' successor governments would still do her bidding in certain particular areas: allow her companies to exploit their natural resources, for example, especially oil; let her keep her military bases, naval facilities and secret listening posts there; and not go over to the Soviet Union. In other words – reverting to the sort of language we usually employ for early-stage imperialism – could she still sustain her *informal* empire overseas? In addition to this, with Britain's and

America's global interests becoming more and more entangled after the War, would the successor states still respect the latter's interests too? That in fact was quite a useful tool for Britain in resisting some nationalist demands, with the US actually supporting Britain's position – effectively bolstering the British Empire, therefore – if they thought it could act as a counter to Soviet influence.[5] This of course was at the height of the 'Cold War', another boulder in the way of the normal downhill rush of the Empire. Nonetheless, there is a certain irony there.

The underlying reason for this decline – or progress, by another way of looking at it – was Britain's lack of power in the world, exacerbated by her lack of will, to pursue the policies that would have been necessary to retain her empire; both of which went back decades. The two world wars, of course, drained her of what remained of the former, which had never been very great, measured in terms of military might. In order to boost that, Britain would have had to entirely revolutionise her whole society: militarising it, for example; hardening it to take 'atrocities' like the Kenya death camps in its stride; conceive of herself more as an 'empire' than that wussy word 'commonwealth'; or, in terms our classically educated schoolboys would have understood, become more 'Roman', and less 'Greek'. There were certainly some people around who were prepared to do that. On the Right of British politics there have always been men (and women, though this is a very 'masculinist' discourse) who went for qualities like discipline, duty, sacrifice, compulsory military service, unquestioning patriotism, toughness, marching up and down, rugger, spending lots of money on battleships and guns, rooting out deviationism, and keeping women in their place, ahead of any of the more namby-pamby liberal ones; and professed to believe, against most of the historical evidence, that these were what had made Britain great and strong in days gone by. An example was 'Mad Mitch', or Colin Campbell Mitchell, the soldier who became a popular hero in the last days of the Aden protectorate, helping to evacuate it, which hit him hard; a great admirer of the fictional heroes of John Buchan and the real heroism of Lawrence of Arabia, until he realised that the latter was a 'practising pervert'; and later resigning his commission and going into Parliament, where he joined the voluble pro-(white) Rhodesian group; but who despaired of the 'old women' (Labour) who had taken over the country from the heroes of old; and always believed that the army was the only 'healthy and virile member' of an ailing national body.[6] Most of those who agreed with him did it from armchairs. (Serving soldiers tend to be less gung-ho.) But there were some, usually ganging up with Rhodesia and apartheid South Africa in the 1960s and '70s; which were the issues that defined them politically, but probably set them against the more dominant political tendencies of the time.

These were proceeding along other lines entirely. They weren't necessarily anti- or non-imperialist. They tackled the problem from the other end. If you couldn't tempt the people away from their liberal values, perhaps you could change the Empire, or even the world, in line with them. The Commonwealth was a stage towards that. So was the

United Nations intended to be. If the latter could forge a new world order in which imperial *rivalries* were kept in check, and whether you were a 'Great Power' or not in the conventional sense didn't matter so much, there was a chance that a 'softer' Britain could still exert an influence in the world that her people could be proud of. Winston Churchill, having come to terms later than most with the end of the Empire as he had known and loved it, believed it could be done by emphasising Britain's *moral* superiority, plus the experience she had accumulated as an imperial power in the past. The United States, having just stepped into her global shoes, should be able to learn from that, surely? Other British politicians, including several of the Labour ones so despised by Mad Mitch, also clung on to this shred. Lastly, there was 'the Bomb' (thermonuclear), which in a way trumped all the other cards in the 'Great Power' pack; first of all by allowing Britain to pulverise any other nation in the world, whatever its conventional military superiority, if she wanted to (and dared to, which she pretty obviously wouldn't); and secondly by allowing Britain (and France, who adopted the same course) into the 'club' of powers that were reckoned to be 'great'. Her bomb's 'independence' was also supposed to qualify Britain's new *de*pendence on America, though it didn't really, because after the early 1960s it relied on American rockets to deliver it.

Still, all this was a way of sustaining a *kind* of imperial status without the bother of having to rule countries; and encouraged Britain, under both shades of government, to continue to assert her right to defend her commercial rights – just those, not colonial – in the world. In a way this should have been a return to her ideal 'free-trade' imperialism of the early nineteenth century: not seeking territory (though that had often come as a by-product) but only free passage for her, and other countries', ships and goods – and in the new age, air traffic and finance. Like the early Victorians, politicians probably fooled themselves about the degree to which this depended on power. In the most notorious episode in which Britain tried to assert 'free passage', through the Suez Canal in the 1950s, she came a cropper when it was resisted by an Arab nationalist government (Egypt), supported diplomatically (this once) by the United States. The 'Suez Crisis' of 1956 has gone down in history as the sorriest example of post-imperial hubris leading to nemesis. It is not a bad moment to choose as marking the symbolic end of the Empire.

Thereafter Britain scaled down her '*East* of Suez' responsibilities, not entirely to the liking of the Americans: the key decision here was a famous Labour Defence White Paper of 1968; and began looking inwards – or Europewards – again. During the late 1960s and early '70s she made several attempts to join the European 'Common Market', as it was called then, only to be vetoed by the French president Charles de Gaulle because he suspected Britain's ties with the USA; which, however, succeeded in 1973, when Britain became a member, albeit an unenthusiastic and 'semi-detached' one from then on. The relevance of this to her imperial history is that it involved her realigning her commercial connections, away from the 'wider world' (including the Commonwealth) which had once comprised the majority of her markets, to concentrate on what before then had been her minority market, the European continent. This is one explanation for the peculiar difficulties she had in adjusting to 'Europe' in the years immediately afterwards; no other member of the European community had had to make a similar switch. It also marked a final rejection of the special relationship she had had for many decades with the Empire/Commonwealth, many members of which felt betrayed. Britain had given up on them.

One remarkable feature of this whole process – decolonisation, disengagement, the turn to Europe – is how relatively smoothly it all went; certainly not in the Empire itself, as we have seen, but within Britain. There were protests, for example in support of the white Rhodesians; some grumbling by Tories and military wallahs over defence cuts; quite a lot of controversy over Britain's entry into the Common Market; and even a political party – the League of Empire Loyalists – set up to try to stop the dissolution of the Empire, and even to seize the colonies back. But the main protests were *anti*-imperialist: in Parliament against the British atrocities in Kenya and elsewhere, for example, when at last they were revealed (they were usually covered up), which was not at all consistent with Britons' cuddly image of the 'Commonwealth'; against Rhodesian racism and South African apartheid; against 'the Bomb'; and against the Suez adventure – provoking the largest popular riots on an issue of foreign policy yet. Otherwise the impact of decolonisation on British society and politics was feeble by comparison with the 'blowback' effect the Algerian wars had in France, for example: although in this connection it may be interesting to speculate what difference it might have made if Rhodesia had been as close to Britain as Algeria was to France. (We shall be coming to a more subtle political effect in the next chapter.) The League of Empire Loyalists was risible. No mainstream party was elected to power because it was 'pro-imperial', and no government removed because of any of these disengagements from the Empire. (Anthony Eden resigned over Suez, but he was ill in any case, and his government simply carried on in other hands.) That must be because the broader population didn't *care* very much about its Empire: either any longer, or perhaps ever.

This should have been the end of it. That it wasn't, entirely, is due to three factors: firstly, the residual imperial instincts in the minds of politicians, especially when they were elevated into positions of power, which have been alluded to already; secondly, the 'liberal imperial' idea that was the most tenacious of those residual instincts; and thirdly, Britain's close – sometimes also referred to as 'special' – relationship with the USA, which sucked her into supporting what came to be regarded as the latter's own form of 'imperialism' (though the Americans vehemently denied this originally), from the later twentieth century onwards.

These factors are all related. If America *was* imperialist, it was in a very similar way to the way Britain had been early in her imperial career, when she had also denied it; that is, as the result of her free trading and liberal principles, rather than for any overtly aggressive and annexationist motives. At various times in the history of the (formal) British Empire, British imperialists had dreamed of integrating the United

States back into the latter, albeit at the price of American leadership, which they were willing to pay; this for example had been one of Cecil Rhodes's great ideas. (It is why 32 out of 52 of his original 'Rhodes scholarships' for colonials to attend Oxford University were earmarked for Americans. Bill Clinton was one. There is an American conspiracy theory that holds that this 'British imperial' connection has secretly driven American foreign policy ever since.[7]) Quite apart from this, the similarities between British and American economic philosophies, by contrast with continental Europe's – the former more 'free marketist', at least after 1979 – naturally drew them together. A common language, law and the outward form of their democracies did the same. For those who missed Britain's past imperial 'greatness', joining America was a way in which they could involve themselves in another great empire which they at least part-owned, historically. That would preserve some of their old prestige. Continental Europe tended to disagree: another common way of portraying the relationship, both there and on the British Left, was with Britain cast as America's 'poodle'. But the Americans were happy to go along with this, so long as it served their ends, and Britain believed it served hers. As Tony Blair's Labour government did, very strongly; leading it into what most people now regard as an unwise and 'poodle'-like commitment to an American policy, in Iraq in 2003, which provoked demonstrations in Britain that topped even the Suez ones, and caused arguably more distress in Iraq itself, and elsewhere, than the tyranny it had been designed to put down had done. This is one instance where some wise advice from

Britain based on her past imperial experience – historians kept yelling 'Egypt 1882' to Bush and Blair (the parallels were very close) – might have come in useful.

From here on the picture becomes diffuse. In a way British imperialism morphed into the American version, with leadership usually going to the Americans; or else into more amorphous but still powerful forces largely out of the control of either, characterised as 'multinational companies', or 'international capitalism', or the even vaguer term 'globalisation', in one of its forms. By its nature this was not always easy to recognise as 'imperialism', though the new Pope Francis managed to spot it in November 2014, when he warned of the threat posed to democracy from what he called the 'unseen empires' of corporate might.[8] A distinguishing mark of this kind of imperialism was that there was little or no attempt to control and direct it independently of market forces, by national governments (even America's and Britain's) or by democracies; leaving the capitalist 'head' of our old imperial 'monster' to pull the body and tail along on its own. The other, 'feudal' head had shrivelled and dropped off. This of course was a universal trend. All over the world, beginning in dictatorial Chile but with Thatcher's Britain an early conduit too, not only empires but most other kinds of political power were giving way to uncontrolled market forces: 'back to nature', as free-trade zealots would have seen it; with 'privatisation' spreading everywhere, even in admired Social Democratic Sweden, and to nearly every area of life. The movement has been so inexorable as to make one suspect that it really *is* a 'natural' one, just as Marx predicted, but possibly without his 'natural' corrective – internal collapse of the system provoking a successful revolution of the proletariat – for its victims to look forward to. Whatever the reasons for this may be *other* than the Marxist one, which looks pretty sound at present, there can be no doubt that the development of capitalism has been the dominant factor in human history over the last two hundred years, easily outranking 'imperialism', whose role was either to ride it (head number one), or to try to head it off (head number two), unsuccessfully in the end.

The British Empire's 'decline and fall' was probably inevitable, therefore, and beyond the 'will' of the British to prevent it, even if they had all been as hard and patriotic and disciplined as Mad Mitch's beloved Argyll and Sutherland Highlanders were. From its very origins it had been built on a misunderstanding: that imperial power, formal or informal, could be exerted cheaply, so as not to hamper enterprise, and liberally, so as not to offend against most Britons' most fundamental values, which were not in fact hard and patriotic and disciplined. Bearing this in mind, it is surprising that it lasted as long into the twentieth century as it did, and not surprising at all that British governments failed in the main (though not always) to achieve the smooth and consensual end to it that they hoped would justify it retrospectively. Nor is it surprising, in view of the work that went into trying to justify it, that some of its features lingered on long afterwards. Eden's and Blair's hubris was one of those features. Others will be explored in the next chapter.

EIGHT

Legacies

T HE PLAN OF MAKING the Empire seem to 'die well', and to Britain's credit, in order to justify it in retrospect, wasn't an unqualified success. Too many of the people who had called for its end had done so because they fundamentally disapproved of it; more, certainly, than those who saw decolonisation as the apogee of the whole enterprise, intended all along. The process of decolonisation was far too messy in places for the idea of a smooth and peaceful transition – a 'transfer of power', as it was called for India – to seem totally credible, and it came to appear even less so when, very late on, official papers that had been hidden away from historians (and of course the wider public) in order to preserve the 'smooth and peaceful' image, leaked out and revealed the true scale of the atrocities that were sometimes resorted to in the course of it. This affected perceptions of the Empire's legacy, its effects on the post-imperial world. Most people painted this negatively, especially those who didn't really know very much about it. Later, when the dust had settled, the Empire gathered some retrospective champions. One of these claimed that the British Empire had 'made the modern world', no less.[1]

In fact both sides may have been mistaken, at least to an extent. One alternative reading hinted at throughout this book is that really the British Empire, *as* an empire, was much less powerful than it is usually taken to have been, from which it follows that it was less responsible – directly, that is – for what happened in its wake. (Of course, you could say that it was morally responsible, by letting it happen, when it was *supposed* to have had control over it.) Many post-imperial developments, including 'making the modern world', might have happened anyway, and possibly with less damage being done to its victims or beneficiaries by not having 'modernity' forced on them imperially in the way it was. Japan and modern China are examples: modernising in their own ways, without any obvious 'Western imperialist' help. Economic development and even democracy, in forms better suited to them, could have grown naturally from elements in other cultures too, and been accepted with better graces, therefore, than their imposition by aliens almost inevitably entailed. (No one likes being told what to do by outsiders. As it happens, I prefer Sweden's form of democracy to the British, but would bridle if a bunch of Swedish imperialists tried to force it on us.) As historians are always taught, as one of their fundamental lessons: *post hoc* does not always mean *ergo propter hoc*; and it certainly did not in the British Empire's case. Many of the post-imperial things that have been either debited or credited to it were not really its doing. The trouble is, of course, that because they happened at the same time, it is often difficult to tell.

There are a few exceptions. The territorial residue left by the Empire, of course, is one. This ranges from uninhabited islands, like South Georgia; several naval stations, including Gibraltar; a lump of the Antarctic continent; through to the troublesome Falklands (Malvinas). Most of these are now classed as 'British Overseas Territories' (before 2002 as 'dependencies'); because they didn't – and still don't – want to join nearer neighbours, and are too thinly populated to survive as nations on their own. Some are valuable to rich Britons (and others) as tax havens. One has kinked the International Date Line so as to make itself popular as the first place to celebrate the new year. The others are more trouble to the British government than they're worth.[2]

A more serious legacy of British imperialism was many of the *frontiers* it left behind. Notoriously in the Middle East, but also in many parts of Africa (West Africa, the old Sudan) and the Indian subcontinent (Kashmir), the present-day shapes of the nations that succeeded the European empires were largely determined by Western rather than local rationales, motives and rivalries, mainly artificially if judged by ethnic, cultural and religious criteria, and as a result have been sources of conflict, some of it very terrible, right up to the present day. Whether the Middle East would be more stable and peaceful today had it not been the subject of Western imperial interference is unknowable – it wasn't always peaceful before; but it is indisputable that the particular forms of the conflicts that have ravaged that region since the post-World War I settlements – for example, those involving Israel – owed much to its European-imposed cartography. This could be said to be the major legacy of British imperialism insofar as international diplomacy is concerned. Of course, it wouldn't have been if the new nations had been able to agree to adjust their frontiers among themselves; but that was probably too much to expect. 'Giving up what one has is always a bad thing', as Queen Victoria once wrote.[3] If it was difficult for her, it will have been more so for the Empire's successor states, which simply had to make the best – or worst – of what they had. Nothing illustrates better the unwisdom of imposing structures on other peoples, even with the best will in the world (which was not always the case here), and so the almost inevitable downside of this kind of imperialism.

Thirdly, there is obviously no disputing the legacy of the British Empire on those parts of the world largely populated by Britons: on the United States of America to an extent, although the signs of British influence there have diminished over time (the oddest manifestation of it is probably the 'Daughters of the British Empire', 'a national philanthropic American Society of women of British or British Commonwealth birth or heritage' dotted all over North America); and in 'white' Commonwealth countries more generally. Visitors to Australia and New Zealand are constantly reminded of it: the Queen on their coins; little Union Jacks sewn into the corners of their flags; university architecture copied from Oxbridge – though you find this in the United States too; the pageant of *British* history

portrayed in one of Sydney's main shopping malls; 'croco-
diles' of young girls in school uniforms and straw hats, last
seen in England *circa* 1960; powerful trade unions – what
can be more British? – and of course pubs. In Canada and
South Africa the British influence is relatively less, due to
rival identities competing with it: French and American in
Canada, Dutch and native African in South Africa. In the
minority white settlement ex-colonies – Zimbabwe, Kenya,
the West Indies, Ireland – it manifests itself in versions of
'Britishness' that seem old-fashioned and relatively less
liberal by comparison with the metropole, affected by the
decades of siege the 'Brits' there have had to endure, or feel
they have. Of course, none of this would have come about
without the British Empire. As neither, probably, would the
spread of English as the second language of almost everyone
in the world, although the monolingual Americans may
have had more to do with that.

A fourth clear legacy of the Empire is cricket. It cannot
be coincidental that the game of cricket is mainly played
today in ex-colonies, whereas the equally British game of
football followed trade. (The point about cricket is this:
imperialists, being gentlemen, were mainly batsmen, and
so needed natives to bowl at them. That's how the latter
learned. Cricket is also a subtle and complicated game, and
so requires decades of colonial tutelage to graft it on, at least
in its early stages. Association football was carried elsewhere
by train drivers and such. It is also much easier to learn.)
Cricket caught on as much in non-settlement colonies as
in Australia and South Africa, and indeed the international
game today is dominated in many ways by the Indians and

Pakistanis the British taught the game to. (And it was the great Indian batsman K. S. Ranjitsinhji who gave the world the leg glance, possibly the most subtle and beautiful of all batting strokes. Australia's contribution has been 'sledging'.) Other examples of visible British 'remains' in the former dependent colonies are the outward forms of certain colonial legislatures; relatively few buildings, compared to those the Romans left, the best of them, however, adapted to native tastes: New Delhi, Victoria Station in Mumbai, the Raffles Club in Singapore, and much of present-day Simla in the Himalayan foothills; some statues of the old Queen and other notable Brits, where they have not been pulled down in anger; British graveyards and war memorials, usually overgrown; and – again – pubs. Correlli Barnett claimed that the army was just about the only British institution to leave a 'permanent mark' in the colonies, in the shape of 'order and organization amid a carnival of collapsing par-liamentary government'.[4] The Ugandan dictator Idi Amin was certainly keen on the uniforms. (He wore a kilt.) But these may be relatively trivial. They don't compare with some of the other modern legacies that have been claimed for British imperialism: like the present disposition of the Middle East; capitalist exploitation; communal animosi-ties; world poverty; third-world homophobia; and racism, especially in Britain itself.

It is these areas where it is usually difficult to disentangle a distinctively *imperial* impact from other more general ones. Of course, yet again, it depends on your definition of the word. If it is stretched so far as to embrace 'Westernisation' it might work for most of them; but even here one would need to be careful not to assume that 'Western' values and practices are or were 'Western' alone. Some of those who attribute 'modernisation' exclusively to the West seem to be blind to how 'universal' and rooted in other societies many aspects of modernisation are; such as – claims the historian Jack Goody – freedom, capitalism, individualism and the rule of law, which are all found in ancient China and India too. Pre-empting these for the West is a kind of cultural theft (one of Goody's books is called *The Theft of History*),[5] and of course muddies the picture of Western imperialism's impact on the world considerably. It also may have a more serious implication, as we shall see shortly.

With the British Empire specifically there is another difficulty; which is that Britain sometimes sought deliberately to obstruct 'Westernisation', if she mistrusted modernity itself, as many of her rulers in the field did, representing the 'feudal' head of the monster; or because she feared that putting Western ideas into native minds might make them less easy to control. We should not forget formal imperialism's – that is, imperialism defined more narrowly – ambivalent relationship with expansive and exploitative capitalism in the nineteenth and twentieth centuries: riding this much more powerful engine sometimes; often trying to put the brakes on it; but usually not in much of a position to do either – where, for example, Britain had 'privatised' her colonial responsibilities in one way or another.

Lastly, there is the issue of unintended effects. This is important if we want to reach moral judgements – though that isn't really a historian's job. It is sometimes assumed that it is malevolent intentions that invariably produce male*ficent* results; but that is clearly not so. Sometimes, in fact, the most benevolent of intentions can turn out badly – usually through bad *judgement*. 'Reformers' aren't aware of the 'latent functions' performed by primitive customs they wish to abolish, and so do more damage than they can possibly realise, through prejudice, stupidity and lack of sensitivity. Early-twentieth-century anthropologists who invented the concept of 'latent function' attributed the demoralisation and decline of whole peoples to this.[6] In another form, it can be seen in the aftermath of the 2003 Iraq war, where the US government's palpable mistakes clearly arose out of a similar mindset. Of course, that war can be put down to other motives entirely: in a word, 'oil'; but it doesn't require a belief in that to explain either the war itself, or the mess it left afterwards. It could have been entirely idealistic (which of course it wasn't), and still been a disaster for the Iraqis; and all those others in the Middle East and elsewhere on whom its effects reverberated. A British imperial example is the Indian 'Mutiny'. It's a pity that Tony Blair was obviously not sufficiently knowledgeable of the history of British imperialism to be able to warn his American allies of that in the case of Iraq. Well-meaning people can do immense harm, as well as duplicitous rogues. That is Blair's situation. Today he cuts an Elizabethan, or even Jacobean, tragic figure. One day a new Shakespeare may do a kind of justice to him.

Most of what has happened in the world since the fall of the British Empire has been due to a complex of factors, of which 'imperialism' was just one – or rather, three or four, depending on the type of 'imperialism' involved. Others include, one has to say, the policies, successful or not, of the governments that inherited Britain's ex-colonies, working of course with the materials left behind, which varied widely – some had viable civil services, police forces, democratic procedures, and the like (India was probably the best endowed); others hardly anything at all, except what was rummaged up in the very last moments; and often under pressure from powerful outside agencies, like multinational businesses, or bigger neighbours, or religious jihadists, or one or other of the 'Cold War' alliances; but all now morally responsible for their own actions and circumstances, to some extent. As time went on, and the formal British Empire receded further into history, one would have expected its contribution to all this to diminish too. But it didn't. One reason for this was the impact of a *myth* of imperialism on the world thereafter, which was arguably at least as important as the material effects of the thing itself. (It often is. Look at the myth of the American Revolution.) That is not in any way to exonerate the British, whose fault it was that this myth had just about enough genuine traction to hold. But for whatever reason, the myth was powerful internationally in all kinds of ways from the 1970s onwards; a new lease of life for British imperialism; its real, albeit ghostly – *pace* Lenin – 'final stage'.

Some features of the myth were spelled out in the Introduction to this book: in a nutshell, the venerable, deliberate, powerful, heroic, racist empire 'on which the sun never set', as imagined by many contemporary imperialists and anti-imperialists, certainly; but, as we have seen, highly flawed. So where's the harm in that? Well, maybe there is very little. It can annoy serious historians, obviously, but do the rest of you need to bother about them? The question is 'merely academic', after all. But it may not be. Myths can have positive effects. There's an episode of *The Simpsons* where Lisa (the bright one) discovers that the foundation myth of her town, revolving around the heroic deeds of Jebediah Springfield ('a noble spirit embiggens the smallest man'), is invented, and resolves to spill the beans at the great town carnival held to honour him, only to have second thoughts at the last minute on reflecting that 'myths bring out the best in us'.[7] Maybe it wasn't such a bad thing, in the immediate aftermath of decolonisation, for the British, too, to have had some myths to make them feel better about themselves; apart from the wartime ones, that is. 'Never mind the history; feel the myth.' In fact there was little sign of mass post-imperial demoralisation in Britain after the fall of the Empire, as we shall see. But this could have been a reason.

On the other hand, myths can also have very negative impacts. Two well-known ones involve the Americans, among whom the idea of a great, powerful British Empire appeared to be particularly widespread, for obvious historical reasons. It had two major (albeit contradictory) repercussions. One was to give the United States something to define herself *against* – the nation's origin was an anti-colonial rebellion – which made it difficult for her to see herself in 'imperial' terms. 'We don't *do* empire', as Donald Rumsfeld once famously said (just before invading Iraq);[8] which only makes any sense at all if you restrict your idea of 'empire' to the formal. By defining their national identity against this 'other' of the British Empire, as they (mis)understood it, Americans blinded themselves to what was undoubtedly imperialistic in their own international conduct. (This self-delusion was in fact quite extraordinary. In 1812 the USA launched one of its many imperial wars, against Canada. In popular American mythology, however, that has become the 'Second War of *Independence*' from the British.) In fact the US pursued policies in the world in the nineteenth and early twentieth centuries which came very close indeed to what in Britain's contemporary case is always *called* 'imperialism'; if Rumsfeld had had a better idea of that latter kind of empire he might have been able to learn some lessons from it. Instead he took another 'precedent', from one of America's 'good' wars: the liberation of Paris in 1944, with American GIs being welcomed joyously by girls and women waving flowers. That is what he confidently predicted in Baghdad; with of course disastrous results. Without this huge blind spot, about the nature of the British Empire, it may not be too fanciful to speculate that the USA might have at least thought twice about repeating Britain's colonial mistakes in Iraq. (This is where a Blair with a degree in History might have helped.)

In another neck of the American 'Neo-Conservative' woods, however, dwelt those who did recognise the imperial analogy, and actually embraced it. They wanted America to follow in Britain's tracks. What 'Afghanistan and other troubled lands today cry out for', wrote one of them in 2001, was 'the sort of enlightened foreign administration once provided by self-confident Englishmen in jodhpurs and pith helmets'.[9] Quite apart from the historical howlers involved here – the British did not actually rule in jodhpurs: they were for playing polo in; and of course never in Afghanistan, where they nearly always struggled militarily (not in polo), and were often repulsed, just like the Americans – the problem with this view is that it gives far too much credit to the *capacity* of the British to do 'good' in this way. In both these cases we can see dangerous practical conclusions being inferred from this overblown myth of the old British Empire.

It can do harm in other ways. One is by tarring certain ideas, especially 'liberal' ones, as 'imperialistic' when they may not be (or not entirely). That is how the African Anglican churches often paint the generally more liberal English Christian view of homosexuality, for example: as a kind of Western 'imperialism' being imposed on them from Canterbury. Whether that is a genuine reason for their homophobia may be doubted (after all, African homophobia clearly has indigenous roots too; and there *is* that bit in *Leviticus*); but it resonates among ex-colonial subjects. In Uganda homosexuality itself is portrayed as a Western imposition – before the imperialists arrived all Baganda were 'straight'. In confusing contrast to this, some ex-colonies, like Jamaica and India, blame their *anti*-gay laws on the British. (The truth is more complex. There were sex laws implemented in some colonies, but usually – as in Britain before 1885 – directed at sodomy, between men and women too. And, again, there was enough prejudice against this kind of thing among native populations not to make such laws exactly an imposition. And lastly: the Jamaicans and others have had more than fifty years to un-impose them, if that's what they think.)

Similarly, President Mugabe of Zimbabwe garners votes by claiming that criticism of his imperfect regime is a cover for a British plot to re-annex his country. Most toppled African dictators raise the same canard. Almost every day fundamentalist Muslims can be found hurling the 'imperialist' charge against people who object to certain practices, like gender segregation, in English Muslim schools: 'an attitude not dissimilar to how the colonial masters dealt with the restless natives' (that was a Birmingham teacher in May 2014);[10] or (more seriously) female genital mutilation. In their case it may seem 'a bit rich', as the saying goes, to excoriate the 'West' for imperialism in view of Islam's own aggressively imperialist past, and even present, in the form of the so-called 'Islamic State' today (2015).[11] The more general case was also sometimes made, as here by a Sri Lankan in 1999, that 'human rights […] are not absolute […] They are relative to the culture. The present day human rights are relevant to the present West, which has been successful in establishing their hegemony over the entire world to a large extent.'[12] That was reason enough to reject them. (The trouble is, there's some truth in it.) Clearly 'extreme' Islamists feel the same. Again, whether Western imperialism and its associated myth were *responsible* for this widespread rejection of liberal values by these groups and others cannot be said for sure. But they surely haven't helped.

That is why it cannot be a bad thing to confront these myths head-on; and in particular the one big myth that lies behind them: which is that the British Empire was sufficiently powerful, committed or long-lasting to leave either all the good legacies, or all the bad, that have been attributed to it. To some readers that may appear to be trying to wriggle out of my own national responsibility for its evils, or (if they are old-fashioned patriots) to deny the Empire credit for the good it did. We shall return to this general question, especially of retrospective 'responsibility', in the final chapter.

Before that, and because it bears on this, we must look at what the receding Empire left behind in Britain itself. There its impact was substantial, but not altogether what one might think. We have seen that decolonisation didn't cause much of a political upset in Britain, in the sense of people's resisting it with any great force or effect, or the pattern of party politics being greatly disturbed. The Empire was remembered, sometimes nostalgically, in feature films and television series depicting the old Indian Raj, in particular, in rose-tinted – but not necessarily uncritical – terms, and later in documentary series, usually judgementally 'balanced' to one degree or another; but presented as an exoticism, hardly related at all to the lives and experiences of the vast majority of people who watched them. (Who in the 1980s could possibly identify with the Charles Dance character in *The Jewel in the Crown*?) Of course, there were old colonial hands around, usually living in retirement in the Home

Counties, if they weren't young enough to be redeployed
as (for example) university registrars, with vivid memories
and regrets of their own, but not usually making much of
a public impression beyond the correspondence columns of
The Times and the *Daily Telegraph*. You would also find them,
clustering together for moral comfort, in London Clubs
and on Oxbridge High Tables. They felt undervalued and
besieged in a country that had very rapidly become post-
and even anti-imperial while they had been busy winding
the Empire down. They were rather mocked by the rest of
British society, especially among the young (my generation), albeit sometimes affectionately, as in the character
of 'Major Bloodnok' in the popular BBC radio comedy
series *The Goon Show*; the television series *Ripping Yarns*;
and, even before that, David Low's 1930s cartoon character
'Colonel Blimp', made into a popular film in 1943 which
Churchill tried to ban. This image of the typical 'imperialist'
was widespread in British culture right through the period
of decolonisation, making it difficult to summon up any
support or deep affection for their creature. It was after all
not the 'people's' empire that had gone; never had been, in
the present writer's view.

Responses to tests of 'patriotism' almost never featured
the Empire as a reason for the British or English to feel
proud of their country, even when they took on board past
history. One particularly fulsome celebration of Englishness,
which appeared in a tabloid newspaper in June 2014 (not
Britishness, because it was written in connection with the
World Cup, where the nations are represented separately,
and only England was this time), listed England's military

achievements, together with her cultural and sporting ones (the cultural were a surprise in the *Sun*); but only those in defence of her own 'freedom' – against the Spanish Armada, Napoleon and Nazism, for example; and never in conquering others.[13] After 1945 it was the Battle of Britain that essentially defined her national identity in the eyes of patriots, so far as conflict was concerned, and emphatically not the battle of Plassey, or the Arrow War, or the relief of Mafeking; let alone the campaign against Mau Mau or the battle of Crater – 'Mad Mitch's' last *Boy's Own Paper* fling. Anyone who really believes that modern British nostalgia (of which there is plenty about) has much to do with the Empire should take a look at the British films, TV dramas and documentaries that were made during this period, right up to the present, where World War II must outnumber 'imperial' themes by at least twenty to one: the dominant 'defence of liberty' trope again. It was probably lucky that British pride did have the recent memory of this genuinely heroic event from a 'good' war to sustain it while the Empire was crumbling around it, to somehow compensate. The French had nothing like it; which may be why they seemed, from the contemporary political ructions that events in Algeria and Indo-China provoked, to miss their empire more.

That, however, was not the end of it. The fall of empire could have been reflected in more hidden and subversive ways: in Empire-related values that continued on afterwards, or were suddenly challenged when their imperial supports dropped away. Among the former is often taken to be British feelings of 'superiority' over foreigners, which are supposed to have been one of the factors behind Britain's initial reluctance to join the European Union (under whatever name), and her 'semi-detached' relationship to it even after 1973; and behind the 'racism' that liberals widely deplored in Britain from the 1950s on. There can be no disputing either the Euroscepticism or the racism, of course; but it may be too much of a leap to attribute either of these discourses to Britain's former imperial role, when the latter was (and is) at least as strong in non-imperial and more parochial countries, and there were more immediate and material explanations for both. Europe was, as we have seen, an uncomfortable fit for Britain economically, in terms both of her trade and her dominant – more American – economic ideology; and the substantial immigration of ex-colonial subjects into the United Kingdom, starting in the 1950s – and unprecedented since the East European Jewish influx of the turn of the twentieth century, which had nothing at all to do with empire, of course, but provoked similar reactions – is a far more likely explanation for 'racial' antipathy. To attribute these to attitudes carried over from imperial times is another example of the *post ergo propter* fallacy. At the very least, the connection should not be assumed. It could even be that Britain's imperial experience made those sections of her society least materially threatened by mass immigration, and in the long run, *more* accepting of the 'multicultural' society that was one of the plainest legacies of the Empire to Britain than might otherwise have been the case. They certainly accepted the immigrants' food. ('Chicken Tikka Masala' is apparently now regarded as a traditional 'British' dish.[14]) But then that had very little native competition.

The real lasting domestic repercussions of the Empire and decolonisation, however, were more subtle and indirect. Here the 'hybrid' metaphor used at the start of this book may be worth recalling, in order to explain them. That described a 'monster' (which is not to imply that its disposition was necessarily unrelievedly monstrous), with two heads, a body and a tail. The body was the bulk of the British population, largely unconcerned with the Empire, and certainly not one of its main drivers or agencies. The two heads represented the political classes, one of them old-fashioned and 'feudal', the other more modern and 'liberal', in an economic sense. The second drove the expansion of empire, for profit; the first sought to control it, for the colonial people's good. These reflected the two major tendencies in British domestic society and politics throughout the nineteenth and twentieth centuries, which also divided single parties: the Liberal party in the early twentieth century, for example, and the Conservative party during most of the post-World War II years. Margaret Thatcher famously characterised the 'feudal' members of her cabinets – paternalists and welfarists, successors of Harold Macmillan – as 'Wets', which presumably made those of her persuasion – red-in-tooth-and-claw free marketists – the 'Dries'. Her period of power saw the beginning, at least, of the 'drying out' of British politics, with welfarists both of the Right and the Left marginalised; hence seeming to bear out Marx's prediction (again) that capitalism could not be modified or have its edges softened in the long run, to the chagrin of those of us who had hoped it could. This followed swiftly on the fall of the directly ruled Empire, which could be regarded, in intention at least, as welfarism or paternalism on a broader scale, and may have helped sustain the 'Wets' in the Conservative party, who were also, of course, imperialists. The removal of the imperial plank undermined that tendency in British politics; with domestic political repercussions that we can see today. Now the monster is left with only one breathing head. *Post hoc ergo propter hoc*, I realise; but it fits.

Not that everyone saw the implications of this. The 'drying out' process should have made Thatcher, and the Labour relative free marketists who succeeded her, into anti-imperialists, on old Cobdenite lines; but it didn't. That may have been because, for the political class – and it alone, virtually – the awareness of past national 'greatness', coupled with the 'habit of authority' that comes with exerting or influencing it, gave them delusions of grandeur beyond Britain's present ability to make a mark on the world stage; resulting in, for example, their maintenance for many years of a military establishment much larger than most other nations', and interventions like those in the Falklands (1982) and Iraq (2003). Both of those looked as though they were harking back to imperial times; though it may be significant that the propaganda for both of them emphasised, again, the World War II trope more: 'defending' and 'liberating' peoples from modern-day 'Hitlers'; which was reasonable in the first case – Galtieri was the aggressor, after all; it really was wrong to see this as 'colonialism', just because the Falklands was effectively still a colony – and understandable, though misleading, in the other. In connection with foreign affairs in general, Tony Blair also believed that Britain's imperial *experience* should count for something, like an ex-football star turned coach; which might have been a fair argument if he had used that experience more wisely.[15] Blair was a much more convincing 'imperial' relict than Thatcher, in the 'liberal-imperialist' mode; but then as a Labour leader he had more of the old 'paternalistic' monster's head on him. As well as these big examples there were some more pathetic ones: individual upper-middle-class men soaked in imperial values at their public schools, and in the previous generation's gung-ho juvenile literature, going off on little neo-imperialist jaunts of their own, as mercenary commandos in Africa and elsewhere. (The old Etonian adventurer Simon Mann is a good example.) In all these cases we can see the hubris of empire leaving its mark.

So, however, did the tail of the beast. Albeit often put into the shade by the more spectacular impact of 'jingoism', opposition and indifference to empire had been long traditions in British history; and they, too, were prolonged into the late- and post-colonial eras, with powerful demonstrations against Eden's Suez adventure in 1956, for example; the Vietnam war, strengthening Harold Wilson's resolve not to be dragged into that like Blair was (willingly) into Bush's Iraq war later; South African apartheid, though that wasn't Britain's direct colonial responsibility any more; 'UDI' in Rhodesia, which was; and Britain's co-invasion of Iraq, which provoked the biggest demonstrations on a foreign policy issue ever seen in Britain. By the 1970s, if not before, almost everyone in Britain seems to have been an anti-imperialist, at least overtly, certainly if the complaints of the remaining old imperial fogeys are anything to go by. ('Country gone to the dogs. No pride in the Empire any more. Political correctness gone mad. Pass the gin, old girl.'[16]) Where the fogeys were wrong was in thinking that any of this was new. As we have seen, anti- and non-imperialism were as much inherited from imperial times as was the imperial mindset itself. This may explain why radical opposition to other countries' imperialisms was so powerful in Britain, too.

Other domestic legacies of imperialism are more difficult to unpick. A good case can be made for the Empire's having made things too easy for the British economy in earlier days, by furnishing it with 'softer' markets than she would have to struggle for later, and so contributing to the decline in the efficiency and productivity of British industry that was widely noticed – and possibly exaggerated – at the time. But there are, of course, alternative explanations for that. (The Conservatives liked to blame the trade unions.) An effect of the *loss* of the Empire may have been to take away an important link binding Scotland with England – the Act of Union of 1707, after all, had been largely motivated by a desire by the Scots to participate in Britain's colonial enterprises after the failure of their own, and Scots were always more proportionately involved in the British Empire than the English – leading to Scotland's failed, but close, independence bid in September 2014. Many of Britain's more draconian policing and security methods were pioneered and tested in the colonies (and Ireland) before gradually being allowed to displace her more traditional liberal forms of policing and counter-subversion in the twentieth century; a trend that is still continuing (surveillance, phone-tapping, secret courts, and the like), although as with other similar modern developments the imperial responsibility for this thins out as the Empire is left behind, and other factors (like terrorism) hove into sight. This is one area where the 'feudal' head of our hybrid does still seem to be breathing, albeit softly; more or less dominating the murky – but perhaps necessary – world of Britain's secret services. (That is, until they are 'privatised'. It has happened elsewhere.) Some quite recent heads have had colonial experience. MI6 also retains a quasi-imperial influence outside. 'The last penumbra of empire', was how its deputy chief described it to the Queen in the 1990s.[17] In which case it must be regarded as a 'legacy'.

As must the suspicion attached to Britons abroad at the present day, quite apart from in the ex-colonies; the barbs that most of us who live abroad for any length of time are subjected to, usually in jest, but with maybe a mild sting to them, which one imagines will take some time to disappear. (Modern-day Romans don't seem to suffer in the same way.) This is not new. One of the major effects of the Empire on Britain while it lasted was to make her mistrusted. 'Why did the sun never set on the British Empire?' runs the old Irish joke. 'Because God didn't trust the Brits in the dark.' He still doesn't. The opprobrium arising from her imperial past that still attaches to Britain abroad, whether that is justified or not (and this book may give some clues here), may cling to her for a long time yet. It could require an extended period of decline and disintegration, so that Britain is no longer recognisable as and identified with the Britain of yore – no longer exists, perhaps, as a political nation – for her to be loved again, for herself. It is arguable that that process has already started. In the meantime I'm still tarred with the imperial brush by my friends in Sweden. It's a heavy burden to bear; though not to be compared, of course, with the lasting burden – as well as benefits, like cricket – the Brits may have bequeathed to many of their old colonial subjects.

NINE

Conclusions

EXPANSION IS NORMAL. It may even be 'natural'. Everything – the universe, fauna, flora, us, capitalism – grows, until it dies. Nations and peoples, too, if they can. It is what makes competition and conflict 'natural', as well. In the very long run it may be essential to our species' survival, when our sun dims and Earth becomes uninhabitable. That may be the ultimate answer to the question posed by my interrogator at that party in Nacka a year or two ago: 'Why did you *want* an empire?' But of course it is not a very helpful one, in this specific context. In particular: it does not explain why Britain especially – albeit not alone – expanded in the eighteenth, nineteenth and twentieth centuries; how she expanded; what she did with the countries her expansion spilled into; and why that expansion was as half-hearted as it was throughout most of this period. Added to which, growing and dying are not the only things that 'things' do. They also evolve.

This short book has tried to shed some light on all these aspects of modern British imperialism. If it raises more questions than it answers, then so be it. That should be one of the roles of serious and critical history: firstly to undermine wrong, simplistic or misleading answers ('myths'); and then to show how complex and ambivalent the remaining alternatives generally are. Frustrating though this may be, confusion and complexity are generally a truer way of looking at things than certainty and simplicity; and also safer, in all kinds of ways.

The foregoing chapters are full of the former – complexities, uncertainties, vagaries, even contradictions; which makes it difficult, of course, to sum them up in any kind of 'Conclusion' of the conventional kind. I have no overall 'theory' to explain why the British Empire rose and fell, or generalisation to offer about the way it was ruled. *Except* for one: that both were relative, in all kinds of ways: to British society at any one time, and especially the stages of its socio-economic development; to the contemporary international situation; and to the particular circumstances in which British imperialists and others found themselves in each of their colonies or foreign spheres of influence, almost irrespective, in this case, of the social and ideological milieux they had come from. Hence the confusion; but it should be a confusion the general nature of which is not difficult to grasp.

The first thing to grasp is that there were many kinds of British 'imperialism', all with different motivations and impacts, and including some that at the time were not usually counted as 'imperialism' at all. There were also other forces at work contemporaneously with 'imperialism' which became tangled up with it, but had nothing essentially to do with it, and had motivations and effects of their own. One was the evolution of capitalism, probably the most powerful material force in modern world history, even inevitable – or so it seems now, in the days of its near-universal triumph; with which formal British imperialism had an ambivalent relationship, and which may have been at the root of many of the events that are commonly attributed to 'imperialism', sometimes with – but also often without – the latter's help. Of course, this distinction largely depends on semantics, the great bugbear of modern discussions of the phenomenon: that is, what is *meant* by 'imperialism'? – to which there is no authoritative and objective answer, and so no reason in logic for not defining the word broadly, to include phenomena like the expansion of capitalism if you like. In that case, however, it remains important to try to unravel the different strands in what *you* call imperialism, in order to understand it better. There is too little of that in popular discourse these days.

Some distinctions are obvious. The peopling of Australia with British emigrants, for example, had almost nothing in common with Britain's rule – with a very small number of personnel – over countries like India and Nigeria, with different motives informing each of them, and very different outcomes. For Britain's white Australian subjects, colonialism represented a liberation, with most of them (this of course excludes transported felons) becoming far more individually free than their sisters and brothers back in Britain, and at least as free as those – a majority, as it happens – who chose the USA as their new home. To call them colonial 'subjects' seems perverse. For most of Britain's other subjects, however, colonialism meant a *loss* of freedom, new restrictions on their activities; although whether these amounted to as much in practice as they did in theory, or were more onerous than what they had suffered in their pre-colonial societies, could be a matter for debate. Even for the indigenous non-European peoples in Australia, being under British rule was vastly different from being a non-European in, say, tropical Africa: in this case definitely *more* onerous, partly because of the way the Colonial Office devolved responsibility for them onto the more privileged settlers. The same differences were to be found between directly ruled colonies like those in tropical Africa, and the 'privatised' ones like South Africa and Rhodesia. British motives varied according to what they wanted from a colony, and methods according to circumstances. And the word 'British' is misleading, if it implies that these were the same people or class of people in every case. If there was more than one kind of colony, there were many types of colonialist, too. Even among the most imperialist of Britons, there were few who were equally enthusiastic about all species of colony: aristocratic India, for example, as well as democratic Australia. You had to choose.

One of the reasons for this lay in what I have called the 'hybrid' or transitional state of contemporary British domestic society then, with the upper classes in uneasy alliance with the middles, giving rise to confusions, contradictions and tensions within the British Empire throughout its history. One of the main tensions was between the 'paternalistic' tendency in British colonial policy, and the 'capitalist' one – 'tendencies' only, mark: the picture was rarely as clear-cut as this. In very general terms, it was the capitalists who acquired the Empire, and the paternalists who tried, at any rate, to run it. It is easy to see the potential for tension there. Both had their advantages and disadvantages: rapid 'development' and social disruption in the 'privatised' colonies, leading sometimes to 'atrocity'; economic and political stagnation in the paternalistic ones, but with more gentleness. There was almost no agreement within the Empire about what was to be done with its 'natives'. District Officers, traders, concessionaires and missionaries all fought with one another for their own interpretations of their 'duty' towards the Africans, or whomever. The only thing they might agree on – but not always – was that the 'natives' could not necessarily know what was best for themselves.

Another, secondary, complication was the frequent gap between policy, or original intentions, and practice in the colonies themselves; which latter largely depended on conditions 'in the field', which included not only the powers and dispositions of the native peoples there, but also the *functions* of the different groups of imperial agents or actors among them; which was what lay behind those disputes between missionaries, traders and so on. These factors greatly influenced race attitudes, too, probably more than any preconceptions the imperial agents may have brought with them from home, or the 'domestic discourse'. Opinions were fitted to functions, rather than the other way around.

A further distinction is that between enthusiastic 'imperialism', called that, of which there was comparatively little, and opposition to it, or criticism of it, or more often simple unconcern – what elsewhere I have called 'absent-mindedness'–which were at least as common and important in Britain (not to mention in the colonies) during most of the imperial era. The reason for that is that there was a multitude of rival discourses in Britain besides, and usually outreaching, the 'imperial' one. Britain may have been an imperial nation, measured by the actions overseas of her statesmen and businessmen, but was never an imperial *society* to any significant extent. Apathy or a very weak interest also played a part, with Britain – as has been mentioned already – being the first and leading *anti*-imperial nation in the early twentieth century, as well as the dominant imperial one: 'anti-imperialism', that is, being defined as opposition to empire per se, rather than simply to the particular one that was oppressing you just then. This is rarely acknowledged; probably because 'pro-imperialism' made a bigger show. (And because of the myopia of the 'post-colonial' set.) That was another powerful product of her general culture – or, more accurately, culture*s* (plural) – at this time.

Which brings us back to the question: how was it that such a relatively *un*-imperial society could accumulate such a huge empire during these years? There are two answers to this. One is that the British Empire was never quite as 'imperial' as it looked: won partly through luck and the passivity of others in the world, even by 'accident' in some places; ruled cheaply and through collaboration (with settlers or natives); and always vulnerable to the kind of combination of indigenous and international pressures that in fact would only come to threaten it in the twentieth century. One effect of this was that it didn't require a highly imperialised society, willing for example to make sacrifices for it, to hold it up. The second is that society – 'the people' – had very little say. Britain was not a democratic polity, remember, until well into the twentieth century. Even when it became one, or to be called one, it remained fairly easy to 'manage' by certain special interests within it, or even to deceive. 'Democracy' requires transparency to work properly. (It is only today becoming clear how much information about the seamy side of empire was kept from people at the time, and still is being, retrospectively.) Nearly all of these special interests were male, of course: did that make a difference? Or would women placed in the same situations have acted similarly? Of course, there were ways in which the Empire might have affected directly and adversely even those who didn't have the vote, if they were taxed or conscripted into the army to maintain it, for example; which they never were. *Until*, that is, very near the end (the end of World War I was the key moment), when it did need a broader societal effort, and so – partly for this reason – the Empire fell.

It follows from this that while it (formally) existed the British Empire was indeed what Richard Cobden had claimed it was as early as the 1840s, and British socialists also used to believe until fairly recently, when ingenious ways were found of apparently involving 'the people' in it retrospectively: that is, an essentially upper- (and

upper-middle-) class masculine enterprise – what Cobden's
ally John Bright called 'a gigantic system of outdoor relief
for the aristocracy' – expressing those classes' interests and
values above any more democratic ones; and curiously
distinct from the commercial and financial interests of the
classes who were mainly responsible for imperial*ism*, in
the sense of the imperial *expansion* which – *pace* Cobden
and Bright – had brought the Empire about. Imperialism
and the Empire, in other words, reflected the class and
possibly gender divisions that have long lain at the root of
British domestic history, despite repeated efforts by politicians – John Major's and Tony Blair's 'classless societies'
most recently – either to erase or to deny them; certainly to
the present day (this is written in 2014) of 'Bullingdon Boys'
lording it over honest-to-goodness Northerners and Scots.
(In popular Northern and Scottish perceptions, that is.)

That is not, however, to attempt to apportion *blame* for
imperialism; least of all to seek to offload it from the shoul-
ders of the class I may be thought to represent (aspiring
working-class parents, 'rising' through the professional
lower middle class, to lefty intellectual). That sort of consideration should be left out of this kind of discussion. The
upper and middle classes were not to 'blame' for imperialism in any significant sense, any more than the working
classes were for (at the very least) not using the strength
of their numbers to put a stop to it. All of them just did
what came naturally. Behind their individual and collec-
tive motives were forces beyond their control: economic,

social and – some way behind those two, because largely dependent on them – 'cultural'.

The second reason for not wanting to lay blame – or for that matter praise – on too heavily is that it might imply blame- or praise-worthy *motives*, which very often had little to do with the ways imperial policies panned out. Tony Blair once notoriously stated, in connection with his part in the 2003 invasion of Iraq, that it was only the purity of his motives that counted, for which he was answerable to his God alone; whereas of course the democracy to which he was supposed to be politically accountable rates *judgement* more highly, and rightly, because there is no necessary correlation between pure motives and good effects – benevolence and beneficence – at all. Harm can be done with the best of intentions. That was often the case with the British Empire. Which is not *of course* to say that many evil-intentioned – brutal, selfish, dishonest – people were not involved too. The Empire often turned people that way. The same points can be made about nations. It was circumstances that determined whether they became 'imperial' or not. Finland's prime minister once told a visiting Nazi German diplomat that his country would undoubtedly have expanded if the conditions had been right. The possibility, even, that in other circumstances Britain might have followed a path similar to Nazi Germany's in the 1930s is suggested by some of the atrocities that were committed by her own agents in the colonial field. It's not something in the national blood; or even a nation's constitutional arrangements. 'Free' democracies can turn imperialistic, and even atrocious, too.

Nor is it something that is inherited. Even if my 'class' *were* complicit in the imperialism of the nineteenth and early twentieth centuries, that wouldn't involve me, simply because I live on the same patch of ground they did all those years ago, but subjected to very different (in my case lefty intellectual) influences. Too much is probably made, in Britain especially, of 'history' as a determinant of our 'national identity'; which is dangerous if it leads education ministers, for example, to seek to tweak school history courses in order to furnish a narrative consistent with what at the time is viewed as a 'good' identity; and distractive, if it prevents us from building an identity based on our national ambitions, rather than the past. (Sweden does it better: teaches values like equality as the bases of her identity, which certainly don't come from her national history, which has been as problematic as ours.) Imperialism is no important part of the British national present, though it has obviously had its effects, both material and as a source of myths. If it is possible to construct such a thing as a British national identity, then it should be based on our values today. What history may teach us is that this is going to be very difficult, in the light of the fact that there never was a time in the past when all or most Britons, or even English people, shared a common view of their nationality, as opposed to – for example – a class-based one. Late-nineteenth-century efforts by conservatives to use the Empire for this very purpose – to bring the working classes on board *their* patriotic boat – all failed. One must assume that present-day government attempts to do the same retrospectively will too.

As for 'lessons', the other thing that people often expect or want to take from history – well, there are not many, really. There are illuminating comparisons that can be made between British imperialism in the nineteenth century and the American 'superimperialism', as I have called it, that came after; but none of them as positive as certain Americans (and Niall Ferguson) took from them at the time of the 2003 Iraq war. The British Empire can't be emulated because, whatever the parallels, circumstances are crucially different now from what they used to be; and because one of the effects of the former was to prepare people for the latter. ('Oh no, we've seen that before.') The best lessons one can take from the history of British imperialism are probably in the nature of warnings: learning, that is, from its failures and mistakes. We have seen how Bush and Blair might have had second thoughts about their invasions of Afghanistan and Iraq in the 2000s if they had been aware of some of Britain's imperial fiascos in both of those places, and elsewhere; although even in those cases it should probably be said, in fairness, that it didn't follow automatically that trying the same thing again wouldn't work out this time. In very general terms, however, the lesson of history is that imperialism, or intervention that can be portrayed as imperialism, rarely works as it is meant to.

The reasons for this are many, and even obvious. One is the confusion of motives and agendas that invariably accompanies imperialism, which can obscure its aims and consequently complicate its effects. Self-serving capitalists often figure here. (Even if oil wasn't in the front of Bush's mind when he invaded Iraq, it was somewhere there, and didn't help.) A second reason why imperialism doesn't usually work is the (very general) 'law of unintended consequences', whereby even interventions that succeed in their main objects (like toppling Saddam) can give rise to further problems that might even overshadow and negate the original one (Saddam), in ways that are unpredictable – except, perhaps, by close and disinterested students of the circumstances of those places and times. The same of course can be said of most wars. A third reason for the general 'failures' of imperialisms is that they tend to provoke their victims; or even – if you want to regard them in this light – their beneficiaries, simply by being imposed upon them. No adults (and not many children, even) like that. This can be compounded – fourthly – if the imperial agent appears to have little understanding of or sympathy for the societies and cultures it is trying to 'benefit'. This often comes with the self-confidence and power that enable certain nations to dominate (or 'benefit') others, and is compounded by the universalist philosophies that bolster that: the assumption that the former's ways of life and principles of government – Christianity, 'Westernisation', Islam, socialism, democracy, free markets, and so on – are (a) the reasons for their own dominating position; (b) their justification for that role; and (c) equally suited to the societies they are dominating, and so to be spread 'universally', for everyone's good. In Britain's case, as we have seen, this assumption came to be modified in certain instances, partly because of her weakness in 'the field': that is something that *might* be learned from; but even then counterproductively, when colonial subjects quite reasonably suspected the motives behind her new-found 'tolerance' of 'primitive' ways. All this, of course, applies to the more 'benevolent' forms of imperialism. 'Malevolent' kinds – slavery, land robbery, King Leopold II of the Belgians – are even more likely to come to sticky ends eventually. (Most imperialisms are mixes of both.) Which makes this the main lesson to be drawn from the history of British and other modern imperialisms, if there is one: *don't do it*. It usually turns out badly, in one way or another. Any benefit to be gained by the subjects of it is usually marginal, more properly attributable to other contemporary forces and influences, and overbalanced by the evils that inevitably come in its train (or, in the case of 'malevolent' imperialisms, straight away). Even the dominating powers usually come a cropper. Look at Rome, Spain, the Soviet Union, present-day Britain. Their imperialisms helped none of them in the long term.

It is also worth noting that much of this was apparent at the time. British imperialism stimulated, or provoked, a great deal of domestic discussion about imperialism from the later nineteenth century onwards, on all sides of the argument, in a great debate which was on the whole far more sophisticated than the present-day one, and covered many of the problems that seem so new to us today. Chief among these were the problems of 'failed states' and the responsibilities of the rest of the international community towards them; the challenge of Islam; the management of the world's natural resources; economic 'development' and how it should be pursued in 'third world' countries;

the dangers of irresponsible monopoly capitalism; 'universal' human rights and how they should be distinguished from national or cultural preferences and prejudices; the problems of cultural relativism and multiculturalism; and how to police a world full not only of villains, but also of well-meaning fools. If it is difficult to think of events on the ground in the nineteenth and twentieth centuries that could fruitfully be scoured for positive guidance today, there is masses in the critical political literature of the time that might well bear returning to.

An argument can be made out for empire. Of course, it depends on the *type*: whether achieved through conquest and imposition; or by federation and consensus; or (thirdly) by conquest evolving *into* federation – if the last two models can be regarded as 'imperialism' at all. (It rests on the amount and kind of power – 'imperium' – over the others still held by the initiating partner.) The United States of America, the Union of Soviet Socialist Republics, the federation of Yugoslavia and the European Union can be taken as examples of this 'looser' kind of empire, which Britain also sought to emulate in the form of her twentieth-century 'Commonwealth', when her power and sense of moral right to 'dominate' faltered. There could be advantages to this. Economic efficiency is the one usually bruited; but there is more to it than that. It seems to be easier for nations, ethnicities and cultures to live together if power is devolved to someone else, exercising it (ideally) even-handedly, so neutering animosities. Indian Hindus and Muslims lived more peacefully together under the British Raj than before or afterwards. The same could be said for different ethnicities under the USSR and Yugoslavia. Britain's hope for Palestine, during the short period when she had control over it, was that it could be a genuinely multicultural state, embracing Arabs, Jews and Christians, under secular British suzerainty. She professed the same ambition, even, for British East Africa. British politicians always found it hard to see why peoples of different backgrounds couldn't rub along together: a limitation originating, perhaps, in the United Kingdom's own proud tradition as a multinational state – England, Scotland, Wales, (Northern) Ireland – welcome (in earlier times) to all. In most of the parts of the world that have been subject to the most bloody 'ethnic' conflicts in modern times, it has been when the restraint provided by empire – British; Russian; and Turkish and then Serbian in the Balkans – has been lifted. As well as this, over-nationalistic nations – Nazi Germany, for example – can morph *into* empires, too. It seems that, damaging and exploitative as imperialism undoubtedly is, nationalism – usually taken to be its direct opposite and the solution to its problems – can be equally so, in its effects on human lives. That much should be obvious.

Such considerations should not of course be taken to validate British imperialism, even in its more 'liberal' manifestations. If it successfully kept the lid on some ethnic, cultural and religious divisions for the duration, it conspicuously failed to do this in a way that would survive the dismantling of the Empire, which the most liberal of imperialists always claimed to be its ultimate aim, even its purpose, all along. Post-imperial chaos, war and suffering are as much the legacies or 'fault' of imperialism as of decolonisation, and certainly not an indication – *pace* the American Neo-Cons – that imperialism should be reinstated in its earlier guise. Which leaves open the question of how to prevent chaos, war and suffering in the world without the kinds of external intervention that have turned so wrong in the Middle East and Central Asia recently; a genuine problem for those concerned for their fellow men and women wherever in the world they live, and unwilling to let them stew in their own juices. This is especially so for those Westerners who hold that their past imperial adventures were largely responsible for the difficulties these peoples find themselves in: Middle Eastern state formations, for example; which is a flimsy excuse in many cases, and doesn't help. The urge to intervene can be honourable. The problem is how to do this non-'imperialistically'; without, that is, the exploitation at worst, and insensitivity at best, that imperialism usually involves.

One who put his mind to this problem at the height of British imperialism was the economist and journalist J. A. Hobson, whom we have met already; celebrated as one of the great gurus of anti-imperialism, but very far from being an anti-imperialist *pur*. In his case this was because he believed non-imperialism to be an impossibility; if empires no longer took national territorial forms, they could still oppress economically, sometimes quite independently of nations; against which only some kind of external authority could protect their victims. Hobson's alternative to the 'liberal imperialist' solution was a *world* authority, taking the place of existing empires: one that couldn't be hijacked by national or narrow commercial interests, would be able to gain wisdom from a wide range of cultures, and so would act in the interests of the weak as well as the strong. The League of Nations (which he had some part in devising) and the United Nations were supposed to fulfil that role. Something like them is probably still our best hope. (Hobson was a wise old bird.) So far, however, national and ideological rivalries, and maybe the 'natural' urge of certain nations to expand with which this chapter opened, have prevented our current UN from performing this role effectively.

The result is what Hobson feared. The dissolution of the great formal European empires has not had the liberating outcomes many anti-imperialists expected of it. That is because modern imperialism was not a primary agent, the *fons et origo* of most of the effects that were credited – or debited – to or from it, but merely a vehicle for deeper and more powerful forces to gain their ends; *or* – and this is important to note – a way of controlling them. The 'deeper' forces were, of course, those associated with the rise and evolution of market capitalism in modern times, whose overwhelming global victory I could not have anticipated forty years ago, when I wrote my first general history of British imperialism (remember Harold Wilson, and the days of consensus and compromise?), but which seems obvious now – so far. The early stages of its worldwide triumph often (but not always) needed the help of the resources that only nations could provide: diplomacy, armies and so on; which is what originally tied it to formal imperialism, as what Hobson called the latter's 'tap-root'; but in a way that sometimes compromised it, held it back, because of these other attributes of nations: what I have characterised in Britain's case as her 'feudal' head and her critical tail. Formal imperialism was a useful mount for international capitalism for a while, but not an essential one, and occasionally a somewhat froward one; which is why it was not that much of a setback for the capitalists when it stumbled and fell. They simply dismounted and bounded on, under the guise, now, of 'globalisation'. That is why the decline and fall of the British Empire, along with others, has made so little difference to the main dynamic of modern history, to which the Empire, and 'imperialism' in the formal sense, were only temporarily and ambivalently attached.

There is a reason for this, which bears on the question I was asked at that party in Stockholm a couple of years ago. 'Why did you want an empire?' seems straightforward, and is easy to answer in one way: 'Most of us didn't.' That I think is what I replied. But it is also a cop-out, because it doesn't address the assumption that clearly lies behind the question: which is that what we get – what happens in history, in the broadest terms – is generally what we want. That may be a valuable illusion for people to have, if it motivates them to 'want' and work for *good* things: the end of tyrannies, for example; 'peace in our time'; sobriety in 1920s America; a safe haven for persecuted Jews; but it generally isn't true. All these laudable objects in recent history have given rise to evils that were unpredictable, whether or not they outweighed the ones that were laudably and even successfully fought against. Even genuine progress (if we can agree on that) may have been achieved not as a result of the agency of those who campaigned for it, but for other reasons essentially. History – the world – is complicated. Of all general human laws, that of 'unintended consequences' is probably the most powerful; and far more so than the one that always links intentions to effects.

The British Empire was certainly complicated; indeed, a mess. That was both its strength, and the cause of its ultimate downfall. It is also what makes it difficult to analyse, but more interesting to try to, than if it were as straightforward as some more simplistic accounts of and glib references to it make it appear. And that's to look at it merely from the imperial side, the stock end of the gun, so to speak; or, if you think it deserves a softer metaphor, the teat. Its impact on its victims, or beneficiaries, was even more complex, affected as it was not only by the nature of Britain's imperialism, but also by the conditions in which it operated, and the positive agency of its subjects. (That's often forgotten. They were not 'victims', or 'beneficiaries', alone.) An examination of those would furnish the other half of Britain's imperial story. That may be more important, and what this book should have been about. But I made it plain at the outset that it was to be about imperial*ism*, from the metropolitan end, and not the Emp*ire* or the colonies. Those are for others to write about (as of course they have done); but only, I think, after taking the 'ism' on board.

Bibliography and Notes

INTRODUCTION

The best of several recent histories of British imperialism is undoubtedly John Darwin's *Unfinished Empire: The Global Expansion of Britain* (London: Allen Lane, 2012). Readers who have been intrigued by the present book and would like to follow its author's thoughts further can try my substantial *The Lion's Share: A History of British Imperialism 1850 to the Present*, originally published in 1975 (London: Pearson, 2012, 5th revised edn). For a shorter summary (but covering a longer period) W. R. Nasson's *Britannia's Empire* (Stroud: History Press, 2006) is clear and fresh, as well as being written by a 'colonial'. At the other end of the scale is *The Oxford History of the British Empire* (general editor W. R. Louis; Oxford University Press, 1998–9, 5 volumes), which is a valuable compendium of information and approaches to British imperial history. Vol. III (ed. Andrew Porter) covers the nineteenth century; vol. IV (ed. Judith M. Brown and W R. Louis) the twentieth; and there are also several 'supplementary' volumes on various sub-topics, like the 'Black experience', women and the parts played in the Empire by Scotland and Ireland.

A number of television documentaries on the history of the British Empire have appeared in recent years. The best known were written and fronted by Niall Ferguson (*Empire*, Channel 4, 2003), and by Jeremy Paxman (*Empire*, BBC, 2012). The most reliable, however – by which I mean, of course, that its arguments are closest to mine – is by Stefan Piotrowski (*Ruling the Waves*, 2015), and can be viewed online at http://youtu.be/-oM8GAuS_no. (To declare an interest: I'm in it.)

CHAPTER 1: HYBRIDITY

Much of this chapter is based on my own interpretation of British *domestic* history, which is spelled out more in my ill-fated – it didn't really catch on – *Britannia's Burden: The Political Evolution of Modern Britain 1851–1990* (London: Edward Arnold, 1994). On the public schools, the best overall introductions are probably still E. C. Mack, *Public Schools and British Opinion* (New York, 1938/41, 2 vols), and Rupert Wilkinson, *The Prefects* (Oxford University Press, 1964). My *The Absent-Minded Imperialists*, chapters 3–4, contains a great deal on the divide between the different kinds of school.

1   Joseph Schumpeter, *The Sociology of Imperialisms* (1919).
2   P. J. Cain and A. G. Hopkins, *British Imperialism 1688–2000* (London: Longman, 2001).
3   Martin J. Wiener, *English Culture and the Decline of the Industrial Spirit, 1850–1980* (Cambridge: Cambridge University Press, 2004).
4   J. S. Mill, *Principles of Political Economy*, 2nd edn (1849), book 2, ch. 1, section 3.
5   R. Cobden, speech in Manchester, 15 January 1846; printed in *Speeches on Questions of Public Policy* (1870), vol. I, pp. 362–3.
6   Two leading examples are John Newsinger, *The Blood Never Dried* (London: Bookmarks, 2006); and Richard Gott, *Britain's Empire: Resistance, Repression and Revolt* (London: Verso, 2011).
7   Widely attributed to Gladstone, but probably mistakenly. See http://en.wikiquote.org/wiki/William_Ewart_Gladstone.

8   Herman Merivale, quoted in W. D. McIntyre, *The Imperial Frontier in the Tropics* (London: Macmillan, 1967), p. 11.

9   At Edinburgh, by Dugald Stewart, a disciple of Adam Smith; before going on to Cambridge.

10   Thomas Carlyle, *Past and Present* (1843).

11   David Cannadine, *Ornamentalism* (London: Allen Lane, 2001).

12   Fred Anderson, *Crucible of War* (New York: Knopf, 2000), p. xviii.

13   Cannadine, op. cit.

14   G. B. Shaw, *Fabianism and the Empire* (1900).

CHAPTER 2: RIDING THE BEAST

On the diplomatic and foreign policy considerations, see my *Britain, Europe and the World: Delusions of Grandeur* (London: Allen & Unwin, 1983). For the missionary movement, and its ambivalent position vis-à-vis 'imperialism', see Andrew Porter, *Religion versus Empire? British Protestant Missionaries and Overseas Expansion, 1700–1914* (Manchester: Manchester University Press, 2004).

1   See, for example, Lord Newcastle (Colonial Office) in 1862, quoted in J. D. Hargreaves, *Prelude to the Partition of West Africa* (London: Macmillan, 1963), p. 33; and minute by Elliot (Colonial Office), June 1866, quoted in W. D. McIntyre, *The Imperial Frontier in the Tropics* (London: Macmillan, 1967), p. 129.

2   Figures calculated from William Woodruff, *Impact of Western Man* (London: Macmillan, 1966), pp. 314–30.

3   Hilaire Belloc, 'The modern traveller' (1898).

4   See Geir Lundestad, 'Empire by invitation? The United States and Western Europe, 1945–1952', *Journal of Peace Research*, September 1986.

5   A registrar at one of my universities was an ex-colonial civil servant.

6   W. K. Hancock, *Survey of British Commonwealth Affairs*, vol. II, part 2 (1942), pp. 190–1.

7   On this, see my '"Bureau and barrack": early Victorian attitudes towards the Continent', *Victorian Studies*, vol. XXVII, no. 4 (1984); and '"Monstrous Vandalism": capitalism and philistinism in the works of Samuel Laing (1780–1868)', *Albion*, vol. XXIII, no. 2 (summer 1991).

8   See Eric Stokes, *The English Utilitarians and India* (Oxford: Oxford University Press, 1959), p. 19 *et passim*.
9   Occasionally it was simply meant to indicate that a subject of a school history book, for example, would include the other nations of Britain as well as England. Examples are Chambers's *History and Present State of the British Empire* (1837) and Dr Collier's *History of the British Empire* (1858).

CHAPTER 3: IMPERIALISM, LEFT AND RIGHT

There is an extensive older literature examining nineteenth- and early-twentieth-century ideas (and ideals) about empire, going back to A. P. Thornton, *The Imperial Idea and its Enemies* (London: Macmillan, 1959). Among more recent books are Duncan Bell, *The Idea of Greater Britain* (Princeton: Princeton University Press, 2007), and Andrew Thompson, *Imperial Britain: The Empire in British Politics, c. 1880–1932* (Harlow: Longman, 2000) and *The Empire Strikes Back?* (Harlow: Longman, 2005). For many years virtually the only work on 'anti-imperialism' was my own *Critics of Empire* (London: Macmillan, 1968; republished by I.B.Tauris, 2008). Recently, however, that has been supplemented, if not quite supplanted, by Gregory Claeys, *Imperial Sceptics* (Cambridge: Cambridge University Press, 2011); and Mira Matikkala, *Empire and Imperial Ambition* (London: I.B.Tauris, 2011). The 'classic' work here is J. A. Hobson's *Imperialism: A Study* (1902; republished with a new introduction by J. Townshend; London: Unwin Hyman, 1988).

1   Anthony Sampson, *Macmillan* (Harmondsworth: Penguin, 1967), p. 65.
2   Edward Gibbon, *The History of the Decline and Fall of the Roman Empire* (6 vols, 1776–89).
3   Quoted in Eric Stokes, *The English Utilitarians and India* (Oxford: Oxford University Press, 1959), pp. 45–6.
4   Bernard Henry Holland, *Imperium et Libertas* (1901).
5   See J. Ellis Barker, *Drifting* (1901). He also published dozens of articles.

6   Edmond Demolins, *Anglo-Saxon Superiority: To What It Is Due* (1898).

7   For references, see my 'The Edwardians and their empire', in Donald Read (ed.), *Edwardian England* (London: Croom Helm, 1982), pp. 134–5.

8   Lord Curzon, 'The true imperialism', *Nineteenth Century*, vol. LXIII (1908), pp. 157–8.

9   Again, references in my 'The Edwardians and their empire', loc. cit., pp. 130–3.

10   C. F. G. Masterman et al., *The Heart of the Empire* (1901).

11   Tim Jeal, *Baden-Powell* (London: Hutchinson, 1989), p. 392.

12   T. J. Macnamara, 'In corpore sano', *Contemporary Review*, vol. LXXXVII (1905), p. 248.

13   Lord Meath, 'Have we the "grit" of our forefathers?', *Nineteenth Century*, vol. LXIV (1908), p. 425.

14   This was taken from a children's 'ABC' from this period, accompanying a picture of the Queen astride the world. (Africa was hidden under her skirts.) But I've lost the reference, and can't find the book again, despite much hunting. Mary Frances Ames's *An ABC for Baby Patriots* (1898) is similar.

15   It needs to be emphasised here that the Congo Reform Association stood for just that – the 'reform' of colonialism – and not its abolition.

16   J. G. Lockhart and C. M. Woodhouse, *Rhodes* (London: Hodder & Stoughton, 1963), pp. 69–70.

CHAPTER 4: IN THE FIELD

Anthony Kirk-Greene's *On Crown Service: A History of HM Colonial and Overseas Civil Services 1837–1997* (London: I.B. Tauris, 1999) and *Britain's Imperial Administrators 1858–1966* (Basingstoke: Macmillan, 2000) are the latest on this. Of older books, Robert Heussler, *Yesterday's Rulers: The Making of the British Colonial Service* (Oxford: Oxford University Press, 1963) and Philip Woodruff, *The Men Who Ruled India: The Guardians* (London: Jonathan Cape, 1954) are still revealing. For a direct insight into the minds of some of the British rulers of Africa, see Anthony Kirk-Greene (ed.), *Gold*

Coast Diaries: Chronicles of Political Officers in West Africa, 1900–1919 (London: Radcliffe Press, 2000), one of a number of diaries and memoirs that have been published recently.

1   Ronald Hyam, *Empire and Sexuality* (Manchester: Manchester University Press, 1990).

2   John M. MacKenzie and T. M. Devine (eds), *Scotland and the British Empire* (Oxford: Oxford University Press, 2012).

3   Anthony Kirk-Greene, *Britain's Imperial Administrators 1856–1966* (Basingstoke: Macmillan, 2000).

4   I have a file of papers sent to me in the early 1990s by Harold Smith, ex-Colonial Office, testifying to what he claimed was the 'fixing' of Nigeria's first democratic election, and also to widespread sexual abuse of young Nigerian boys by members of the local colonial service in the 1950s and '60s. He failed to arouse the interest of any of the government and media agencies he wrote to at that time. I am told that these papers were also deposited in Rhodes House, Oxford. The first scandal always seemed likely; the second appears more so in the light of similar sex scandals emerging in Britain recently.

5   Malcolm Milne, *No Telephone to Heaven: From Apex to Nadir – Colonial Service in Nigeria, Aden, the Cameroons and the Gold Coast, 1938–61* (Stockbridge: Meon Hill Press, 2000).

6   See Helen Tilley, *Africa as a Living Laboratory: Empire, Development and the Problem of Scientific Knowledge, 1870–1950* (Chicago: Chicago University Press, 2012).

7   Bronisław Malinowski, *The Dynamics of Culture Change* (New Haven: Yale University Press, 1965, new edn).

8   Tilley, op. cit., p. 290.

9   Rudyard Kipling, originally directed to the United States, and entitled 'The white man's burden: the United States and the Philippine Islands' (1899).

CHAPTER 5: HOW IT HAPPENED. BROADLY.

Any of the general surveys recommended above (appended to the 'Introduction') will serve to fill readers in on this. A classic work, and the starting point for any consideration of the 'Scramble for Africa', is Ronald Robinson and John Gallagher, *Africa and the Victorians: The Official Mind of Imperialism*, first published in 1963 (London: Macmillan, 1981, 2nd edn). P. J. Cain and A. G. Hopkins, *British Imperialism*, originally published in two volumes: *Innovation and Expansion 1688–1914*, and *Crisis and Deconstruction 1914–1990* (London: Longman, 1993), describes the economic engine behind imperialism convincingly. The best thing on the 'Great' War and the Empire is Robert Holland's chapter, 'The British Empire and the Great War, 1914–1918', in *The Oxford History of the British Empire*, vol. IV, *The Twentieth Century* (ed. Judith M. Brown and W. R. Louis, 1999).

1   See above, ch. 1.
2   Quoted in W. L. Langer, *European Alliances and Alignments 1871–90* (New York: American Book Supply Co., 1931), p. 308.
3   Ibid.
4   Ronald Hyam, *Elgin and Churchill at the Colonial Office* (London: Macmillan, 1968), p. 251.
5   See my *The Origins of the Vigilant State* (London: Weidenfeld & Nicolson, 1987), p. 169, and references cited there.
6   See, for example, John Charmley, *Churchill: The End of Glory* (London: Hodder & Stoughton, 1993).
7   It was only a hint. See Ian Kershaw, *Hitler 1889–1936* (London: Penguin, 1998/2001), p. 556.
8   Quoted in Peter Fleming, *Invasion 1940* (London: Hamish Hamilton, 1957), pp. 177, 192.

CHAPTER 6: THE EMPIRE AT HOME

The place to start here is John MacKenzie, *Propaganda and Empire: The Manipulation of British Public Opinion, 1880–1960* (Manchester: Manchester University Press, 1984); and also Mackenzie's 'Studies in Imperialism' series (Manchester University Press). These can be followed by my own *The Absent-Minded Imperialists: The Empire in British Society and Culture* (Oxford: Oxford University Press, 2004), where most of the sources for the claims made in this chapter will be found. Edward Said's influential *Culture and Imperialism* (London:

Chatto & Windus, 1993) should also be consulted, though it comes from a very different academic stable ('Cultural Studies'), and sits uneasily with the work of more traditional, or empirical, historians. If readers prefer that approach, Said's book inspired a whole 'school' of what is called 'New' or 'Post-colonial' history.

1   Noël Coward, *This Happy Breed* (1943), quoted in Jan Morris, *Farewell the Trumpets* (London: Faber, 1978), p. 302.

2   John Finnemore, *Famous Englishmen* (1901), pp. 3, 5; quoted by Stephen Heathorn in '"Let us remember that we are English": constructions of citizenship and national identity in English elementary school reading books, 1880–1914', *Victorian Studies*, vol. XXXVIII (1995), p. 417.

3   J. R. Seeley, *The Expansion of England* (1883), p. 10.

4   H. John Field, *Towards a Programme of Imperial Life: The British Empire at the Turn of the Century* (Oxford: Clio Press, 1982), chs 4, 5.

5   For example, by Edward Said in *Culture and Imperialism* (London: Chatto & Windus, 1993), p. 291.

6   See Luis Ajagán-Lester, *'De Andra': Afrikaner i svenska pedagogiska texter (1768–1965)* (Stockholm: HLS Förlag, 2000).

CHAPTER 7: THE BEGINNING OF THE END

The best general surveys are John Darwin, *Britain and Decolonisation* (Basingstoke: Macmillan, 1988) and *The End of the British Empire: The Historical Debate* (Oxford: Blackwell, 1991); W. D. McIntyre, *British Decolonization, 1946–1997* (Basingstoke: Macmillan, 1998); A. N. Porter and A. J. Stockwell, *British Imperial Policy and Decolonization, 1938–64* (2 vols, Basingstoke: Macmillan, 1987, 1989); Ronald Hyam, *Britain's Declining Empire* (Cambridge: Cambridge University Press, 2006); W. R. Louis, *Imperialism at Bay: The USA and the Decolonization of the British Empire, 1941–1945* (Oxford: Clarendon Press, 1977); and the series *British Documents on the End of Empire*, published by HMSO, especially the editors' introductions to Series A, vols II and IV (1992, 2000), by Ronald Hyam and W. R. Louis. On Kenya, Caroline Elkins, *Britain's Gulag*

(London: Jonathan Cape, 2005) and David Anderson, *Histories of the Hanged* (London: Weidenfeld & Nicolson, 2005) are essential if painful reading.

1   H. A. L. Fisher, *A History of Europe* (London: Edward Arnold, 1936/1960), p. 1275.
2   To the South African Parliament, 3 February 1960, and widely reported. 'The wind of change is blowing through this continent. Whether we like it or not, this growth of national consciousness is a political fact.'
3   Philip Murphy (ed.), *British Documents on the End of Empire*, series B, vol. IX, *Central Africa* (London: Stationery Office, 2006).
4   See Calder Walton, *Empire of Secrets: British Intelligence, the Cold War and the Twilight of Empire* (London: Harper, 2013).
5   W. R. Louis and R. E. Robinson, 'The imperialism of decolonization', *Journal of Imperial and Commonwealth History*, vol. XXII (1994).
6   Aaron Edwards, *Mad Mitch's Tribal Law: Aden and the End of Empire* (Edinburgh: Mainstream, 2013), p. 139.
7   Carroll Quigley, *The Anglo-American Establishment: From Rhodes to Cliveden* (New York: Books in Focus, 1981).
8   Quoted in the *Guardian*, 29 November 2014.

CHAPTER 8: LEGACIES

For the latest Anglo-American phase of 'imperialism' (if that is what it was and is), see my *Empire and Superempire: Britain, America and the World* (New Haven: Yale University Press, 2006). So far as the Empire's domestic repercussions are concerned, it may be too early for a scholarly and balanced literature to have emerged, though there have been many superficial attempts, especially in connection with racism and 'national identity'. A more serious start, however, has been made with Stuart Ward's (ed.) *British Culture and the End of Empire* (Manchester: Manchester University Press, 2001).

1   Niall Ferguson, *Empire: How Britain Made the Modern World* (London: Allen Lane, 2005).

2   See Robert Aldrich and John Connell, *The Last Colonies* (Cambridge: Cambridge University Press, 1998).

3   G. R. Buckle, *The Letters of Queen Victoria*, 3rd series, vol. I (London: John Murray, 1930), p. 615.

4   Quoted in Aaron Edwards, *Mad Mitch's Tribal Law* (Edinburgh: Mainstream, 2014), p. 271.

5   Goody's *The Theft of History* was published by Cambridge University Press in 2006. See also his *Capitalism and Modernity: the Great Debate* (Oxford: Polity Press, 2004).

6   On 'latent function', see Thomas K. Merton, in *Social Theory and Social Structure* (1949).

7   The episode is called 'Lisa the iconoclast'.

8   Quoted in the *Guardian*, 2 March 2003.

9   Max Boot, 'The case for American empire', *Weekly Standard*, 15 October 2001.

10   Reported in the *Guardian*, 14 May 2014.

11   See Efraim Karsh, *Islamic Imperialism: A History* (New Haven: Yale University Press, 2006).

12   'The bare doctrine of Blair the bear', *Kalaya*, 28 April 1999.

13   'This is Our England', special supplement to the *Sun*, 12 June 2014.

14   According to the late Robin Cook: speech to the Social Market Foundation, reported in the *Guardian*, 19 April 2001.

15   See for example Blair's speech to the Partnership Summit in Bangalore, 5 January 2002; widely reported at the time.

16   This is made up; but based on personal recollections of Cambridge High Table life in the later 1960s. (Except the 'old girl'. Women weren't allowed on High Table then.)

17   Quoted in Calder Walton, *Empire of Secrets* (London: Harper, 2013), p. 338.

Index

Uganda, 100, 158, 164
Unilateral Declaration of
    Independence (UDI),
    140, 172
United Nations, 69, 138,
    145, 193
United States of America, *see*
    America
upper and upper-middle
    classes, 10, 25–6, 38–9, 44,
    55, 61, 75, 108, 110, 115,
    119, 141, 172, 180, 183–4;
    See also aristocracy; public
    schools
USSR, *see* Russia
utilitarianism, 47, 121

Versailles treaty, 136
Victoria, Queen, 39, 59, 97,
    156, 158
Vietnam, 168, 172
Vikings, 11, 13, 70

Wales, 14, 22, 70, 75
war memorials, 158
War of 1812, 163
Watts, G. F., 124
welfare state, 31, 54, 65, 170–1
Wells, H. G., 62
Wembley, 68
Western domination, 12

Westernisation, 49, 84–5, 89,
    155, 159, 188
West Indies, 44–5, 94–5, 103,
    113–4, 137–8, 157
Westward Ho! School, 78
White Man's Burden, 90
Wilde, Oscar, 63, 125
Wilhelm, Kaiser, 100, 105
Wilson, Harold, 172, 193
women, 56, 58, 64, 66, 68, 72,
    74, 76, 82–3, 104, 117, 131,
    143–4, 183
working classes, 13–14, 16,
    63–6, 75, 79, 84, 98, 102,
    104–5, 107–8, 115, 118–9,
    121–4, 126, 129, 151,
    184, 186
World War I, 67, 103–6, 124,
    129, 134, 136, 143, 156, 183
World War II, 36–7, 70,
    109–11, 133, 137, 143, 163,
    168, 170–1
Wyllie, Sir Curzon, 103

Younghusband, Francis, 102
Yugoslavia, 1901

zenith, 99
Zimbabwe, 56, 139, 157, 165
Zinoviev letter, 108
Zulus, 35